Secular and Religious Dynamics in Humanitarian Response

This book investigates the ways in which the humanitarian system is secular and understands religious beliefs and practices when responding to disasters. The book teases out the reasons why humanitarians are reluctant to engage with what are seen as "messy" cultural dynamics within the communities they work with, and how this can lead to strained or broken relationships with disaster-affected populations and irrelevant and inappropriate disaster assistance that imposes distant and relatively meaningless values.

In order to interrogate secular boundaries within humanitarian response, the book draws particularly on qualitative primary data from the aftermath of Typhoon Haiyan in the Philippines. The case study shows how religious practices and beliefs strongly influenced people's disaster experience, yet humanitarian organisations often failed to recognise or engage with this. Whilst secularity in the humanitarian system does not completely exclude religious participation and expression, it does create biases and boundaries. Many humanitarians viewed their secularity as essential to their position of impartiality and cultural sensitivity in comparison to what were seen as the biased and unprofessional beliefs and practices of religions and religious actors, even though disaster-affected people felt that it was the secular humanitarians that were less impartial and culturally sensitive.

This empirically driven examination of the role of secularity within humanitarianism will be of interest to the growing field of "pracademic" researchers across NGOs, government, consultancy, and think tanks, as well as as researchers working directly within academic institutions.

Olivia J. Wilkinson is Director of Research for the Joint Learning Initiative on Faith and Local Communities. She publishes on humanitarian and refugee response, particularly around the role of local actors.

Routledge Research in Religion and Development
Series Editors:
Matthew Clarke
Deakin University, Australia
Emma Tomalin
University of Leeds, UK
Nathan Loewen
University of Alabama, USA

Editorial board:
Carole Rakodi
University of Birmingham, UK
Gurharpal Singh
School of Oriental and African Studies, University of London, UK
Jörg Haustein
University of Cambridge, UK
Christopher Duncanson-Hales
Saint Paul University, Canada

The *Routledge Research in Religion and Development* series focuses on the diverse ways in which religious values, teachings and practices interact with international development.

While religious traditions and faith-based movements have long served as forces for social innovation, it has only been within the last ten years that researchers have begun to seriously explore the religious dimensions of international development. However, recognising and analysing the role of religion in the development domain is vital for a nuanced understanding of this field. This interdisciplinary series examines the intersection between these two areas, focusing on a range of contexts and religious traditions.

The Sarvodaya Movement
Holistic Development and Risk Governance in Sri Lanka
Praveena Rajkobal

Secular and Religious Dynamics in Humanitarian Response
Olivia J. Wilkinson

Secular and Religious Dynamics in Humanitarian Response

Olivia J. Wilkinson

Routledge
Taylor & Francis Group

LONDON AND NEW YORK

First published 2020
by Routledge
2 Park Square, Milton Park, Abingdon, Oxon OX14 4RN

and by Routledge
52 Vanderbilt Avenue, New York, NY 10017

Routledge is an imprint of the Taylor & Francis Group, an informa business

First issued in paperback 2021

British Library Cataloguing-in-Publication Data
A catalogue record for this book is available from the British Library

Library of Congress Cataloging-in-Publication Data
Names: Wilkinson, Olivia J., author.
Title: Secular and religious dynamics in humanitarian response /
    Olivia J. Wilkinson.
Description: Milton Park, Abingdon, Oxon ; New York, NY :
    Routledge, 2020. | Series: Routledge research in religion and
    development | Includes bibliographical references and index.
Identifiers: LCCN 2019041914 (print) | LCCN 2019041915
    (ebook) | ISBN 9780367188337 (hardback) |
    ISBN 9780429198618 (ebook)
Subjects: LCSH: Disaster relief. | Humanitarianism. |
    Humanitarianism—Religious aspects. | Disaster victims—
    Religious life.
Classification: LCC HV553 .W53 2020 (print) | LCC HV553
    (ebook) | DDC 363.34/8—dc23
LC record available at https://lccn.loc.gov/2019041914
LC ebook record available at https://lccn.loc.gov/2019041915

ISBN: 978-0-367-18833-7 (hbk)
ISBN: 978-1-03-208350-6 (pbk)
ISBN: 978-0-429-19861-8 (ebk)

Typeset in Times New Roman
by Apex CoVantage, LLC

Contents

Acknowledgements

I completed this research while affiliated with two main partners. First, I give my sincere thanks to everyone at Trinity College Dublin, including those at the Irish School of Ecumenics, particularly Dr. Iain Atack and Dr. Carlo Aldrovandi for their supervision during my PhD, and those at the Trinity Long Room Hub and the lifelong friendships made there. Second, an abundance of gratitude goes to Jean Duff and Stacy Nam at the Joint Learning Initiative on Faith and Local Communities (JLI). Jean has been a mentor and an inspiring champion of the need for research in this area. The primary research was supported by the Irish Research Council and the book process by the JLI. Thank you for help from Helena Hurd and Leila Walker at Routledge.

I am immensely grateful to all those who I got to know in the Philippines and everyone that helped with the research. I think of the people in focus groups who had deep concerns to get off their chests or just those who enjoyed having a place to talk, the humanitarian workers, some of whom took me in at various times when new typhoons came through and I was in between accommodations, and the local faith actors who showed me what it means to care in a demanding, compassionate, and all-in way.

I thank my family and friends. My parents-in-law for their loving support, particularly letting us take over their home (and their office space) in the final month of writing. My parents and brother for supporting all points in my education that led to this place. My husband, Aaron, has been with me on all stages of this journey as my debater, my editor, and my equal. This book would not exist without him.

***

I have used sections, with some amendments, from my sole authored 2018 journal article, titled "'Faith can come in, but not religion': secularity and its effects on the disaster response to Typhoon Haiyan," published in Wiley's *Disasters* (2018, VOL. 42, NO. 3. © 2018 The Author(s). Disasters

© Overseas Development Institute, 2018. Published by John Wiley & Sons Ltd, 9600 Garsington Road, Oxford, OX4 2DQ, UK and 350 Main Street, Malden, MA 02148, USA).

Ideas in Chapter 5 are derived in part from an article published in the Journal of Contemporary Religion, 2018, VOL. 33, NO. 2, © 2018 Informa UK Limited, trading as Taylor & Francis Group, available online at www. tandfonline.com/doi/full/10.1080/13537903.2018.1469260.

Acronyms

BEC	Basic Ecclesial Committee
CAFOD	Catholic Agency for Overseas Development
CBCP	Catholic Bishops Conference of the Philippines
CSO	Civil Society Organisation
DRR	Disaster Risk Reduction
DSAC	Diocesan Social Action Centres
FBO	Faith-Based Organisation
FGD	Focus Group Discussion
HQ	Headquarters
IASC	Inter-Agency Standing Committee
ICRC	International Committee of the Red Cross
INGO	International Non-Governmental Organisation
IOM	International Organisation for Migration
LGU	Local Government Unit
MSF	Médecins Sans Frontières
NASSA	National Secretariat for Social Action
NGO	Non-Governmental Organisation
NNGO	National Non-Governmental Organisation
OCHA	United Nations Office for the Coordination of Humanitarian Affairs
SRP	Strategic Response Plan
UN	United Nations
USAID	United States Agency for International Development

1 Introduction

Why secular-religious dynamics matter in the humanitarian system

I was sitting in a café on an island in the Visayan region of the Philippines in 2015, waiting for an interviewee to arrive. It was about 18 months since Typhoon Haiyan hit and you could mostly no longer visibly see the effects of the typhoon in this area. My interviewee arrived a little late and apologised – they were working for a large and well-known secular humanitarian organisation in a community-facing position and were constantly busy. They were from another region in the Philippines and knew the Visayan region well. They voiced dissatisfaction with the humanitarian response and then went on to explain that, of course, they frequently brought up religion in their work with communities, just because it was part of life there.

Jump back a few months before and I was in a Western European country talking to an international humanitarian worker who had just come back from working on the Haiyan response. They explained to me that, as they work for a secular organisation, faith does not come into their work at all. Then they followed up by saying that, anyway, they were brought up in a Catholic school in Europe and so they "get" religion in the Philippines. They were mostly perplexed as to why I would ask about this subject.

These two staff members worked for the same secular humanitarian organisation, although different branches of it and I have no reason to believe they ever interacted. These two divergent perspectives represent two ends of a spectrum that we will call the secular-religious dynamics of humanitarian response. What is notable about these two responses is that both felt that their way of working was obvious. On the one hand, religious belief and practice were clearly part of humanitarian action for the humanitarian worker from the Philippines. On the other hand, religious belief and practice were clearly not part of humanitarian action for the humanitarian worker from Western Europe. And even if they were, they knew the main tenets of Catholicism, which is the majority religious tradition in the Philippines, and so they would know if there was reason to bring religion up.

I present these two responses as opposites not because every international humanitarian worker said the same thing, or every local and national worker reiterated a similar point. Other people questioned and subverted these modes of thought, acknowledging that there were secular-religious dynamics that they struggled with, asking what they should do about it, and wondering how to overcome divides that they perceived.

After studying the effects of secularity on humanitarian response for half a decade, the familiar narrative I hear among international humanitarians (that are not explicitly faith-based) is that religious beliefs and practices are overall a negative for humanitarian response. There has been, and is growing, debate about the pros and cons of religion in humanitarian response. I will sum them up without further ado. Faith-based actors in humanitarian response are positive because they allow for improved access to remote areas through religious networks, they are first – and last – responders, they have trust and authority in their communities, and they provide spiritual and communal support for improved coping during and following crises (Ager *et al.* 2015). Some of the usual negatives cited are fears of proselytising and conditional aid, a lack of technical capacity, especially a lack of familiarity with humanitarian principles, and the influence of religious positions on harmful social norms (e.g., gender inequality) and in conflict dynamics (religious actors as parties to conflict) (Wilkinson 2018a). There is no overarching, final conclusion that faith-based actors are more or less effective than others (Tomalin 2012). Yet the final, but arguably the most influential and little discussed, point is that secular perspectives in humanitarian action are not neutral either. The contribution of secular aspects to the secular-religious dynamic is understudied, meaning that the current state of the field has focused more attention on debates about the added value of faith-based approaches to humanitarian action, or critiquing the effects of religious beliefs and practices in humanitarian action. This leads to an imbalanced perspective that has overly wrought the significance of religion rather than holding the complexity of secular-religious dynamics in perspective and understanding that secularity has, equally, its opportunities and challenges and is intertwined with religious elements that make the isolation of religion, and faith-based organisations, unhelpful. The rest of this book delves into that point.

Why does analysing the secular in humanitarian response matter?

This book presents an analysis of the ways in which secular-religious dynamics affect international humanitarian response to disasters, using evidence from the response to Typhoon Haiyan in the Philippines and drawing further insights from the workings of the humanitarian system as a whole. The inspiration came from my own initial forays into humanitarian research, when I had the startling realisation that people went out of their way to avoid discussing "messy" cultural aspects of humanitarian response, such as how disasters affect people's religious beliefs and practices and how those same religious beliefs and practices affect the humanitarian response. The stakes can be high when these aspects are ignored, with misunderstandings leading to strained or broken relationships with disaster-affected populations and irrelevant and inappropriate disaster assistance that imposes distant and relatively meaningless values on people that are in need.

Why are some secular humanitarians scared of the subject of religion? Or, more alarmingly in some ways, why do they simply not care about this subject? I have come across senior humanitarians who have stated that secular-religious dynamics are not important for humanitarian response and then, within almost the same breath, listed the ways in which beliefs and practices have affected their operations recently. What is the effect of this secularity on humanitarian recipients? It appears that pervasive secularism in the humanitarian system has served to marginalise religion so thoroughly that it has become, at best, forgotten and, at worst, taboo and hidden. The dynamics of proselytising humanitarian organisations have also served to make many humanitarians forcefully anti-religion, believing that their secularity ensures their impartiality and neutrality in comparison to the biased and unprofessional beliefs and practices of religions and religious actors. I have equally heard time and again from faith-based humanitarian actors that they completely reject proselytisation, as seen in the ways in which they are hyper-vigilant about maintaining their impartiality and neutrality.

Despite a recent surge of academic interest (Ferris etc.), with recent additions in the area of the history of humanitarian action as related to Faith-Based Organisations (FBOs) (Curtis 2018; Freeman 2019; King 2019), weaknesses remain in both academic and practical understanding of secular-religious dynamics and the humanitarian system. For several years, scholars have called for an analysis of secular values over an essentialised, myopic focus on religion in humanitarian and development research (Fountain 2013b, p. 9, 2015, p. 91). Away from the purely academic, organisations are also lagging behind in their engagement with this dynamic. Consultations have pointed towards the fact that there is a lack of religious literacy among policy makers and warned against an "add religion and stir" model of religious engagement and inclusion in policymaking (Wilson and Mavelli 2014). Many barriers remain and previous reports have highlighted the need for further research into "conflicting secular and religious world-views" (Fiddian-Qasmiyeh and Ager 2013).

Much of the debate so far has been conceptual and theoretical. This is one of the few pieces of research that specifically analyses empirical findings on secularity in humanitarian response. By grounding the work in empirical data, I am able to show that the secular is a resonant concept for study in humanitarian response and that the application of concepts from the sociology of religion such as secularisation theory and post-secularism can clarify some of the forces at work in interactions in humanitarian settings around the world.

This book is about the secular but also necessarily therefore about religion and ranges of how religious and secular beliefs and practices affect each other. I propose that the post-disaster context provides a uniquely clear example of when relatively delineated (or as far as the two can ever be delineated) versions of secular and religious expressions meet, precisely because the need for humanitarian response is defined as the point at which the local and national systems to respond to crisis are overwhelmed and external, frequently Global North, actors arrive to assist. Many of these organisations originate from largely secularised countries yet work in more religiously-centred cultures around the world (Barnett and Stein 2012, p. 23; Ager and Ager 2015, p. 9). The post-disaster environment signals a convergence of worldviews and power plays between external and internal actors (Merli 2012, p. 28). Secular and religious beliefs are one way in which worldviews can differ. The post-disaster environment provides a place for the religious and the secular to work together, which may lead to challenges as well as opportunities both for those providing humanitarian assistance (aid organisations) and those receiving it (the beneficiaries). There is a broad range of organisations present in the humanitarian sector, from those directly inspired by faith to those who maintain a strictly secular approach. Yet there is an inherent assumption that the secular is the default and the faith-based is the deviation (Barnett and Stein 2012, p. 22). Ager and Ager (2011) call this the "functional secularism" of the humanitarian community, implying that the secular is seen as the norm to be attained and maintained. Others have stated that this dominant secularism constitutes "an ontological injustice, where both alternative non-secular visions of the world and visions of alternative non-secular worlds are subordinated to secular ontologies" (Wilson 2017, p. 1). A focus on the secular in research on humanitarian action is innovative in that it illuminates what can be particularly and peculiarly seen as secular in the humanitarian system, whereas much of the previous research in this area has focused on what can be particularly and peculiarly called faith-based or focusing on the influence of religion and more broadly on development work, rather than specifically humanitarian action (for example, G. Clarke and Jennings 2008; M. Clarke and Halafoff 2017; Tomalin 2013a, 2015; Heffernan *et al.* 2009; Bush *et al.* 2015b).

While this research process has shown the ways in which the humanitarian system does work effectively based on the constantly negotiated, micro-level interactions between humanitarians and crisis-affected people, international, national, and local staff, those with fervent theistic and atheistic beliefs and everyone else somewhere in between, these processes are *ad hoc*, unrecognised, and unsupported. Acknowledging that there are many success stories with the slow and almost imperceptible navigation of potentially highly sensitive terrain thanks to the work of individual staff members and community leaders that act as culture brokers, it remains the case that secular-religious dynamics can be a factor that have the potential for serious effects on a humanitarian response. For example, Fiddian-Qasmiyeh (2011) gives an example of tense and unforthcoming relationships between secular and faith-based organisations in Sahrawi refugee camps, to the extent that the beneficiary population have learned and worked within these tensions between the International Non-Governmental Organisations (INGOs) by presenting themselves in the required fashion according to differing Non-Governmental Organisation (NGO) worldviews, even altering religious practices (or at least pretending to). In another example from Burchardt (2013) in South Africa, evidence from research shows that FBOs must live up to the institutionalised secular standards of the international system. Fiddian-Qasmiyeh, this time with Ager (2013, p. 29), also offers another angle in which organisations could miss important elements of aid provision if not religiously and culturally aware:

> As the Tsunami struck in the early morning, women were dressed in whatever they were wearing indoors. . . . Some of them were very, very unhappy with the way that service delivery was provided: having to line up, and stand in a queue without having a headscarf to wear was very uncomfortable for them. . . . It was very important, when we were designing what we call "dignity kits" or "hygiene kits," for us to put scarves in the kits.
>
> (Stakeholder Interview, Henia Dakkak, UNFPA)

These are but a few examples that show not only that organisations can inadequately acknowledge religious experience and well-being within humanitarian programming but also struggle to engage with other organisations due to differing secular or faith-based outlooks. This is a struggle noted not only between the secular and religious but also across the international humanitarian system, which fails to recognise "the underlying structures and assumptions" that lead to prejudices and biases that ultimately challenge improved engagement and partnership with local and national actors, as well as beneficiaries (Bennett 2016, p. 4). It is a system that operates according to its own international standards and has trouble relating to local contexts and realities, meaning that it comes across as out-of-touch, inappropriate, and even neo-colonial in its perceived Westernising agenda. For the successful implementation of humanitarian strategies, programmes must be culturally appropriate and relevant to the affected communities (Oliver-Smith and Hoffman 1999, p. 11; Patterson *et al.* 2010, p. 132). Problems and mistakes will occur if they are not (Lin and Lin 2016). The implication for secular humanitarian actors is that religions should be acknowledged as significant for a large number of their beneficiaries and that programmes will not be relevant or appropriate if it is not recognised that their secular background may be biasing their understanding of this dynamic.

The influence of biases is strong. An international humanitarian in the Philippines once told me that, "There's a perception that 'religion' will be troublesome, but all would say they try to be culturally sensitive," demonstrating the tensions between perceptions and the gaps in accepted norms, such as cultural sensitivity. It is the influence of unconscious biases that is often the most significant. People say that they want cultural sensitivity, but then they repeat words and actions that undercut this ideal, not realising their own biases about religious beliefs or practices. There is a fundamental lack of examination of the effects of a secular-religious dynamics on the relevance, appropriateness, and effectiveness of an organisation's programmes in highly religious contexts. As such, this book is also a critique of the power imbalances in the international humanitarian system, discussed as broke and broken (Barder and Talbot 2016), in need of reform, and insufficient for the ever-growing levels of need around the world.

Overall, I do not find that secularity in the humanitarian system completely excludes religious participation and expression. Instead, secularity is about boundary-making, about carefully demarcating what aspects of religion are allowed in a secular, humanitarian public sphere and what aspects are disallowed and should therefore be ignored, discouraged, or banned using secular justifications. Secularity is demonstrated by a secularised (non-transcendent) morality and ethical structure, strict prohibition of proselytisation, a secularised mission and vision for organisations, the dominance of bureaucratic methods focused on efficiency and with a material focus, the marginalisation of discussion about secular and religious dynamics sometimes to the point of religion as taboo, a secularised workplace so that religion is privatised to an activity outside the workplace, a belief that secularity leads to superior impartiality for humanitarian work, and demonstrations of the power of secularity by defining the boundaries at which religious beliefs and practices are accepted or not within a frame of respect and cultural sensitivity, which can, however, lead to instrumentalisation of religion for other ends. Particularly related to efficiency and impartiality, beneficiaries of humanitarian assistance characterised traits of secularity with many of the effects of distancing and bureaucratisation, namely short timelines for assistance, a material focus, a lack of interaction, and a lack of impartiality and trustworthiness. Chapter 2 details the theory behind these points and Chapter 4 provides empirical evidence.

Conceptual background: secular and religious dynamics

Defining the secular, and secular-religious dynamics, is a necessary part of this picture. Just as with religion, it seems that most of us have a relatively quick definition at hand about what constitutes the essence of "secular-ness," usually along the lines of it being the opposite of religion. But, as we start unravelling it further, Charles Taylor's pronouncement on the subject is understandable; as he says, "I have been struggling with the term 'secular,' or 'secularity.' It seems obvious before you start thinking about it, but as soon as you do, all sorts of problems arise" (Taylor 2007, pp. 14–15). The Oxford English Dictionary has 19 definitions of the word secular. Two themes are common throughout these variations: first, that the secular pertains to that which is not religious and is therefore this-worldly; second, and relating back to its Latin root (*saeculum*, meaning an age or period), the secular can refer to something that is of an age and therefore very long-lasting (indeed, an eternity for the human mind). From both definitions, the concept of the secular as being very much of the human world emerges. The secular is not merely the negative definition of what is without religion but a vastly expansive maze of concepts about what it means to be of this world – temporal, material, and profane.

When it comes to religion, finding a one-sentence definition is problematic. Some classic definitions have been much debated (for example, Geertz 1993), some scholars push for "common sense" short definitions (Bruce 2011a), and others argue that religion is too diversified and "historically specific" to define (Asad 1993) in a globally pertinent and meaningful manner. Definitions of religion mostly fall into those that describe religion in a functional manner (what it does) and those that give a substantive definition (what it is) (Tomalin 2013, pp. 52–55). Wilson points out that the meanings of "religious" and "secular" have subtle differences "from religion to religion, denomination to denomination and congregation to congregation" (Wilson 2012, p. 40) and that "understandings of religion are not fixed. Understanding of what is religious and what is secular are constantly negotiated and renegotiated, depending on social, historical, cultural, political, geographical, economic, and religious context" (Wilson 2012, p. 62).

While Chapter 3 will outline some of the main aspects of religions that are important in relation to disasters, I espouse Tomalin's position that religions (religious beliefs and practices) should be used in the plural to show that there are a "variety of 'religions' that do not neatly fit universal definitions" (Tomalin 2013, p. 51). Likewise, as a sociologist, it is not my position to advocate for a secular or religious position, but to consider religions, and I would add secularities, "as an important and significant variable while also being aware that the form and structure that [they] take may vary considerably across diverse traditions and contexts" (Tomalin 2015b, pp. 68–69). Mostly, as will be explained in the next sections, the main concept in this book is to interrogate secular-religious dynamics together, rather than apart. Yet, on the occasions that they can be isolated, the parameters outlined in what follows further define the particularities of secularities in which we are interested.

The main parameters of secular forces

To pinpoint the main features of secular-religious dynamics for humanitarian response, theories from secularisation, post-colonial critique of the secular, and critique of the secular in international relations are useful. To add a quick note on language, I use the terms secular, secularity(/ies), secularisation, and secularism. These are all distinct concepts. Secularism mostly refers to political secularism related to nation states and is less frequently a topic of concern in this book. Secularisation is what happens at a societal level in terms of increased secularism and secularity, so in the humanitarian system we are interested in secularising processes at a more concentrated scale. "Secular" is the adjective but can also be used to denote "the secular," and secularity is the norms and dispositions that characterise the secular. These are the most common terms I will use to denote secular aspects of the humanitarian system.

As a first point of contact, the ideas from secularisation theory help provide some of the strongest parameters. The process of complete secularisation (that religions will diminish in significance to the point of eventual disappearance) has been largely set aside (Berger 1999; Habermas 2008; Martin 2010; Casanova 2019, pp. 2–3). In its place, scholars now speak of the dynamics between and across secular and religious beliefs and practices, emphasising how political secularism is used and abused against religious minorities (Mahmood 2015), debating the extent of religious resurgence in the modern era (Thomas 2005), considering the place of religion in the post-9/11 world (Lincoln 2006), arguing for religious pluralism (Berger 2014) or multiple ways of viewing modernities around the world (Eisenstadt 2010), and largely settling somewhere in between, interrogating the complexity of intertwined and irreducible secular and religious dynamics (Berger 2014, p. xii; Riesebrodt 2014, p. 3; Casanova 2019, p. 33).

Yet the concepts inherent to secularisation are still relevant to some contemporary societies (Bruce 2011b) and can help pinpoint the main elements of the secular. Original conceptions of secularisation saw the complete decline of religion. Max Weber referred to a process of rationalisation and bureaucratisation at the heart of a decline of religion (Aldridge 2013, p. 67). Many secularisation theories still focus on the decline, decay, and displacement of religion and its authority. Casanova's version of (only) European secularisation (Casanova 2019, p. 2) is that it is

> measured by three different indicators: 1. by the long term relative loss of power and prestige of religious institutions . . . 2. by the general decline in religious practices among the European population . . . and 3. by the perhaps less pronounced, but nonetheless equally noticeable decline in religious beliefs, in the general belief in God as well as in the more specific beliefs in the concrete confessional doctrines of the various Christian churches.

Taylor's (2007, pp. 2–3) group of three includes, 1) the emptying of public spaces so that "economic, political, cultural, educational, professional, recreational – the norms and principles we follow, the deliberations we engage in, generally don't refer us to God or to any religious beliefs," 2) "the falling off of religious belief and practice in people turning away from God, and no longer going to Church," and 3) the pluralisation present in the world today consisting of "a move from a society where belief in God is unchallenged and indeed, unproblematic, to one in which it is understood to be one option among others." Taylor's third point forms the foundation of his argument (2007, p. 437), that

> Religious belief now exists in a field of choices which include various forms of demurral and rejection. . . . But the interesting story is not simply one of decline, but also of a new placement of the sacred or spiritual in relation to individual and social life.

From these considerations, Taylor (2007, pp. 19–20) offers a

> one-line description of the difference between an earlier time and the secular age: a secular age is one in which the eclipse of all goals beyond human flourishing becomes conceivable; or better, it falls within the range of an imaginable life for masses of people. This is the crucial link between secularity and a self-sufficing humanism.

A secular age for Taylor is thus one in which the final and primary goal of life is human flourishing, rather than a flourishing that can be found beyond this life, such as in heaven.

A review of these secularisation theories shows that some common strands emerge that mark the existence of the secular in a given context. The first is the decline (or the state) of religious influence in terms of the standing and authority of religious institutions, the influence religion has on non-religious institutions, and the general decline of religious influence in the public sphere. The second main point is the decline of religion in people's consciousness and practices. Pluralisation of options allows people to think beyond religious influence in their daily lives. These classifications indicate to us that any secular space will have less authority from religious institutions in comparison to other institutions and have other organising principles, ethical and moral structures, not emanating from divine inspiration or aspirations to the transcendent. From these aspects, we can start to see that the international humanitarian system, particularly in its often Eurocentric power structures, might fit within these descriptions as a sphere in which the influence of religion is only one ethos among many and religions do not hold a particular place of authority, although they are present in various ways.

The secular is not neutral

In defining secular parameters, we must acknowledge that they are socially constructed. For example, secularisation is increasingly understood to be an overly Eurocentric idea (or, even more specifically, a *Western* Eurocentric view (Hurd 2007; Casanova 2009, 2019; Mahmood 2015, p. 8)) that does not resonate beyond those borders. Asad robustly critiques the nature of "religion" and the "secular" as used in the West. He describes the secular as one of the concepts central to the idea of modernity as interpreted by those in power in the West. He argues that it is a "project" that "people in power seek to achieve" and has become "hegemonic *as a political goal*" (Asad 2003, p. 13). He wipes the façade of neutrality from the concept of secularism by emphasising that it is closely linked to certain political discourses, notably "the rise of capitalist nation-states," therefore leading him to state that the "secular state does not guarantee toleration; it puts into play different structures of ambition and fear" (Asad 2003, 8). The secular, for Asad, is thus politically motivated, hegemonic, and widely misperceived as tolerant. Mahmood reminds us that "secularism is not simply another term for modernity; it is indexical of those social phenomena, institutions, and practices in which the distinction between the religious and the secular is recurrently salient and often contested" (Mahmood 2015, p. 23). Although

Asad and Mahmood speak mainly of political secularism here, we start to see how secularity in general can be used as a form of constructed power and control.

There has been a struggle in international relations, as equally continues to be the case in humanitarian response, for people to accept that "the secular is not a fixed, natural category, but is socially and historically constructed" (Hurd 2008, p. 13 in Wilson 2012, p. 43). Secularity is a construct that wields power, for those in power, to delineate between what is acceptable and unacceptable. Secularity has a values component that can be forced onto others, just as much as religious belief and practice, which as a social phenomenon is also socially and historically constructed. Mahmood specifies the difference between secularism and secularity on these grounds and how the two are complementary concepts:

> The secular, in other words, is not the natural bedrock from which religions emerges, nor is it what remains when religion is taken away. Instead, it is itself a historical product with specific epistemological, political, and moral entitlements . . . political secularism and secularity. The former pertain to the modern state's relationship to, and regulation of, religion, while the latter refers to the set of concepts, norms, sensibilities, and dispositions that characterise secular societies and subjectivities.
>
> (Mahmood 2015, p. 3)

These critiques shed light on some of the assumptions that may be present in contemporary humanitarian action: 1) that the aim for a society must be a secular conception of "modernity," 2) that the secular is always neutral and tolerant. Likewise, as Field (2017, p. 342) details, two main asymmetries exist in the relevance and appropriateness of humanitarian response: values ("no humanitarian concept or approach is value neutral") and power ("the asymmetry of power and monetary resources in the dominant, international humanitarian system"). The effects of non-neutral values and the power imbalances of the humanitarian system are aligned with the non-neutral and power wielding effects of secularity. We see that secular-religious dynamics are uniquely modern in their way and, as Feener *et al.* put it, " 'religion' is an intrinsic part of the 'secularised' world – not simply a holdover from a bygone era, or an impolite intrusion into a modern landscape" (Fountain *et al.* 2015, p. 20). Equally, this is not to say that the humanitarian system as secular is distinctly modern and the countries in which humanitarian actors work are unmodern. Secularities as sets of socially constructed concepts, norms, sensibilities, and dispositions are the main effect studied throughout the rest of this book. Secularity is not a neutral concept that means the absence of something (namely religion) but is its own web of norms and consequences that affect how people act towards each other and how international groupings, such as the humanitarian system, operate.

Why secular-religious dynamics?

The next step to state, however, is that throughout the rest of this book I will frequently refer to secular-religious dynamics, rather than secular and religious as distinct and clearly distinguishable forces. Just as we see that the secular is not neutral and that it is a product of social forces as with any other organising concept, we are reminded that, "There is nothing new about the copresence of the religious and the secular" (Mahmood 2015, p. 22) as they have come about as coexisting concepts and continue to be so. 9/11 marked a turning point for religion in international relations (Thomas 2005; Lincoln 2006) with scholars arguing for the greater inclusion of thought about secular-religious dynamics in international relations (Fox 2001; Hurd 2007; Wilson 2012; Mavelli and Petito 2014; Rees 2014; Paipais 2018). A binary between opposing secular and religious positions is overly reductive of the intertwined and interdependent terms. To uncover the nuances of humanitarian response, we must use concepts that can cope with more complexity.

The secular and religious are in constant connection with each other. Wilson argues that these binaries must be broken down to engage with the idea that

> the secular and the religious shape and define one another, so that what is considered secular is affected by what is considered religious, secular realms are increasingly influenced and shaped by ideas from the religious, just as religious spheres and actors are increasingly influenced and shaped by ideas from the secular.
>
> (Wilson 2014, p. 235)

She explains that secularism has encouraged an "either/or" model of thinking about religion in which it is institutional, individual, and irrational, without recognising that religion can also be ideational, communal, and rational[1] (Wilson 2012, p. 64). Wilson proposes a concept called "relational dialogism" to denote that there should be a "both/and" approach to secular and religious dynamics, rather than "either/or" (Wilson 2012, p. 95). Within this approach, "the connection between religion and politics within society is viewed not as permanently fixed . . . but rather as a dynamic, fluid relationship, constantly shifting and changing" (Wilson 2012, pp. 97–98). She also notes that it is perfectly applicable to use the relational dialogist model to look at international aid (Wilson 2012, p. 186). Likewise, secular and religious binaries are unhelpful in humanitarian and development settings as, in both the Global South as well as the Global North, it is often impossible to clearly separate the religious from the secular, as people may not think about what they do or what influences them as being "religious" (Tomalin 2015b, pp. 69–70) or "secular."

There is often delineation between humanitarian actors that are faith-based and those that are not, i.e., the secular organisations. FBOs are those whose missions are inspired by faith, who have ties to a religious base or authorities, who may hire staff according to a confession of faith, and who have a significant religious donor base (Thaut 2009; Petersen 2010). The definition of secular organisations emanates from the absence of faith rather than a positive definition of what the secular includes. There is no absolute divide between the faith-based and the secular in humanitarian organisations (Tomalin 2012, p. 693), with many organisations negotiating the space between these categories by maintaining a religious background but operating on the ground according to secular standards (Lynch 2011, p. 221). Thinking about faith-based and secular organisations can be an unhelpful duality because of the scopes of religiosity and secularity demonstrated in many organisations, where there is a co-mingling of both, although it has been argued that there is currently a new "visibility" of faith-based actors in disaster response (Bush *et al.* 2015b, p. 5).

If the secular and religious are so connected, it might seem as though it is unhelpful to distinguish at all. Yet we still see that these concepts, while co-constitutive, can be isolated as particular forces in societies with differing effects on each other, such as the ways in which it is applicable to look at secular-religious dynamics in global contexts (outside of Western Europe alone, and in comparison between Western Europe and other countries). Casanova attests that "global humanity is becoming simultaneously more religious and more secular, but in significantly different ways, in different types of secular regimes, in different religious traditions and in different civilizations" (Casanova 2019, p. 40). He goes on to explain that religious pluralisation has always been a part of globalising forces, just as the changes towards global capitalism and the system of nation states has seen the travel of interpretations of secularism around the world. This has been happening in history and continues to be part of our contemporary global exchanges.

We must see secular-religious dynamics together, but not in conflation to meaninglessness, and hold that these concepts can be used and abused in different ways, in different times, and different places.

In summary, secular forces have certain parameters (lack of religious authority, privatisation of religious beliefs and practices from the public sphere, decline in daily life, the pluralisation of other options), but complete secularisation is unlikely. The secular is not guaranteed to be neutral and tolerant: it is a position created from social, political, and economic forces, just as religious beliefs are seen as a position in this way. Secular-religious dynamics summarise how we must see these as intertwined rather than two opposing categories.

Background on research arenas

The international humanitarian system and its norms are the overarching focus of this book, with specific examples drawn from research following Typhoon Haiyan in the Philippines. The system operates around the world when disasters occur. Disasters happen when interlocking processes of natural or technological hazards combine with socially produced vulnerabilities to create events that overwhelm or completely destroy the essential functions and capacities of a community (Oliver-Smith and Hoffman 1999, p. 4; Wisner *et al.* 2004). When internal capacity is not great enough or sufficiently damaged that it cannot respond to the event, the international humanitarian system arrives with the aim of saving lives, alleviating suffering, and maintaining life with dignity after the disaster.

When speaking of disaster, international humanitarian professionals and scholars in disaster studies use terms such as 'hazards' (e.g., the typhoon), 'risks' (the risk of the typhoon affecting an area), and vulnerability (the weaknesses in social, infrastructural, economic, etc. systems that will make the impacts of the hazard higher in some areas over others). A disaster does not exist through a hazard alone. The hazard must intersect with a community's vulnerabilities to create the disaster. Ultimately, this underlines that the impacts of a disaster happen because of its intersection with society and there is, therefore, no such thing as a purely 'natural' disaster, with the poorest people often the most affected because of their increased vulnerabilities to disaster impacts. There are culturally embedded ways in which people will understand their disaster risks and vulnerabilities. There are a growing number of authors who are engaging with the topic of culture and disaster (Cannon *et al.* 2014; Browne 2015; Krüger *et al.* 2015; Browne and Olson 2019) and the angle I offer is to review the place of secular-religious dynamics within this mix. Just as secular-religious dynamics are socially constructed, disaster impacts result from the combination of hazards and with socially constructed vulnerabilities.

The humanitarian system

Practitioner researchers looking at humanitarian work have, in the last decade, begun to refer to the humanitarian *system* (Walker and Maxwell 2008;

Seybolt 2009; Davey *et al.* 2013). They often characterise this system as complex, displaying the characteristics of non-linearity, emergence, a lack of predictability, and some type of self-organisation. As summarised by Knox Clarke *et al.* (2018, p. 31),

> The humanitarian system is an example of a complex system. It is made up of parts that are at once interrelated and which can also determine their own actions, and which interact with many other elements outside the system. Because it is a complex, open system it behaves in particular ways. It is non-linear: the very large number of interacting elements makes it almost impossible to predict how the system will behave. It is also emergent: as a result of the interactions between the elements, the system itself may develop characteristics which are the result of multiple interactions and are more than the sum of the component parts.

As a system, norms are created and maintained, making it possible for a norm of secularity to become dominant. The system compromises approximately 570,000 staff, which has increased substantially (27% since 2013) in recent years, the majority of the funding flows through United Nations (UN) agencies, and six large organisations dominate nearly a quarter of NGO funding (Knox Clarke *et al.* 2018, p. 16). International humanitarian assistance amounts to US$27.3bn from donors (Urquhart and Tuchel 2018), not accounting for other funds that might help in humanitarian response such as remittances and other social financing mechanisms, including religious tithing in various forms. While there are many factors at play in the international humanitarian system, a review of the "State of the Humanitarian System" in 2018 notes that one challenge of relevance to secular-religious dynamics is "the understanding of, and ability to adapt to, context. The humanitarian system still operates, very largely, according to a standard set of activities, structures and procedures" (Knox Clarke *et al.* 2018, p. 23). While effective in many ways, recent changes towards protracted disasters in different contexts mean that standardised procedures need considerable contextualisation and constant adaptation. Secular and religious dynamics will be part of this context.

Actors in the humanitarian system must negotiate the challenges and benefits of interacting with religions on an almost daily basis. From the surge of evangelical organisations in post-disaster scenarios (Dodds 2010), the security implications of proselytising (Davies 2010), and the perception of humanitarian actors as pushing a neo-colonial/Christian/Western agenda (Ghandour 2003) to the advantages of access to communities through religious networks (Fiddian-Qasmiyeh and Ager 2013) and the support of religious communities for post-disaster psychosocial recovery

(Ager *et al.* 2014), humanitarian actors are unavoidably in contact with religions and their impacts. Some humanitarian organisations seek to distance themselves from religion so as to remain impartial and neutral, two of the main precepts from the humanitarian principles, the fundamental guidelines by which all humanitarian organisations are expected to operate. Others, including some FBOs and religious beneficiaries, may see religion more personally, as a spiritual connection to the transcendent, while yet others might see its importance in the community and for interpersonal relations. In many cases, it is not so much a tension between the secular and religious that dominate but an ongoing intermingling and work from staff to broker between Eurocentric, secular humanitarian modes of practice and daily realities around the world in which secular-religious divides are not as strong and conceptualised in completely different ways. Nevertheless, humanitarian action struggles with broad issues that include religions as an influencing factor: the ongoing debate around the utility of the principles of neutrality and impartiality and the squeezing of "humanitarian space" in which actors are free to work unimpeded (Collinson and Elhawary 2012) as well as the instrumentalisation of humanitarian action for political and military ends (Donini *et al.* 2008) and the question of how to localise humanitarian response. Significant cultural influences, which include the religious, play a part in these imbalances at the core of contemporary humanitarian action (Ager and Ager 2015, p. 9). The tracing of secularity in the norms and trends of the humanitarian system as a whole will be the particular focus of Chapters 2 and 5.

Typhoon Haiyan/Yolanda

The response to Typhoon Haiyan offers an interesting case for this book because of 1) the extremely large international interest and presence of many humanitarian organisations (Escandor 2016), 2) the high level of religiosity in the affected population (Bureau of Democracy, Human Rights and Labor 2013), and 3) the long history of disasters, with the Philippines being one of the most disaster-prone countries in the world (Mucke 2013, p. 9), which has led to disasters being embedded as part of culture and society in the country. Haiyan (locally known as Yolanda) existed for ten days, making landfall over the eastern seaboard of the Philippines on 8 November 2013 (Joint Typhoon Warning Center 2013, p. 47). The strength, speed, and size of Haiyan contributed to its most deadly effect: storm surges. The storm surges produced by Haiyan were up to 6m in height (Ocon and Neussner 2015, p. 10) and hit the shore in tsunami-like waves (Joint Typhoon Warning Center 2013, p. 74). These waves mostly affected the eastern coast of Leyte. The death toll in these areas was significantly higher due to the storm

surges. The city of Tanauan lost 2.74% of its total population (Lagmay *et al.*
2015, p. 9). Local people had experienced many typhoons before and over
125,000 people evacuated from their homes (OCHA 2013a). However,
these tsunami-like storm surges were different (usually the water rises more
slowly and then dissipates). First, flooding predictions underestimated the
possible range of the storm surges meaning that some evacuation centres,
which were officially outside the hazardous area, were inundated. People
had fled their homes only to die in evacuation centres. As Ocon and Neussner (2015, p. 8) put it, "Essentially, the centres became death-traps." Second,
communications about the dangers of storm surges had not been sufficient.
Many did not fully grasp the potential severity of the "storm surge" or what
the term meant and chose to stay put to protect their homes from looting
(Lagmay *et al.* 2015, pp. 10–11; Ocon and Neussner 2015, p. 9).

On November 11th, President Benigno Aquino declared a State of
Calamity (NEDA 2013, p. 2; Hanley *et al.* 2014, p. 18). Haiyan not only
affected the most people of any disaster recorded in the Philippines (over
16 million), but it was also the deadliest event ever to hit, causing 7,354
deaths with many still reported missing (Guha-Sapir *et al.* 2015). The
affected regions are also some of the poorest in the country (NEDA 2013,
p. 16). The majority of the population was dependent on agriculture and
remittances (NEDA 2013, p. 3). With about 600,000 acres of agricultural
lands affected by Haiyan, about three quarters of all coconut crops lost
(NEDA 2013, p. 9), and the loss of fishing boats, motors, and nets, many
families lost their incomes. On November 12th, the UN's "Emergency
Relief Coordinator (ERC) formally activated an Inter-Agency Standing Committee (IASC) system-wide level 3 (L3) emergency response,"
(Hanley *et al.* 2014, p. v) which was the first time an L3 emergency was
declared under a new IASC system. The declaration allowed the rapid
deployment of surge staff to the affected areas (Hanley *et al.* 2014, p. ix)
and the release of resources (US$25 million from the UN Central Emer-
gency Response Fund) (Carden and Clements 2015, p. 3). On December 10th, the UN Office for the Coordination of Humanitarian Affairs
(OCHA) launched its Strategic Response Plan (SRP) (OCHA 2013b). The
total budget requested was US$776 million, which was designed to com-
plement the government-led response, and was 60% funded, receiving
US$469.9 million in total (Financial Tracking Service 2015). The gov-
ernment published their strategic plan for recovery and reconstruction on
16 December 2013 (Hanley *et al.* 2014, p. 18). The government ended
the humanitarian phase of assistance on 4 July 2014 (Hanley *et al.* 2014,
p. 18). The SRP was designed to run for the 12 months following Haiyan,
but since the government declared the initial response to be over earlier,
the SRP ended on 31 August 2014.

Research methodology

In Chapter 2, I draw on existing scholarship to delve deeper into the background to secularity in the humanitarian system. In Chapter 5, I reflect on some of my own recent experiences in policy processes. The primary research following Typhoon Haiyan is mainly represented in Chapters 3, 4, and 5, for which I employed a qualitative methodology, with Focus Group Discussions (FGDs) and interviews serving as the key means of exploring issues of secular-religious dynamics with members of the affected population and NGO staff. Eighteen FGDs with 209 people were spread across the Visayan region (the area impacted most by Typhoon Haiyan), taking place on the islands of Cebu, Leyte, Panay, and Samar. The FGDs were convened with partner organisations. The participants were all adult beneficiaries of humanitarian assistance. To mitigate the potential bias of organisations' selection, I organised FGDs through different organisations (both secular and faith-based) to triangulate different opinions. In data analysis, I also compared results between those organisations that had helped organise the group sessions and other organisations to exclude bias towards the organisers. The qualitative methodology served to allow space for people's reasoning and helped mitigate the effects of sample bias by understanding the range of opinions present.

I conducted 55 interviews with NGO staff from 25 different secular (17) and faith-based (8) organisations to ensure that I was talking to a mix of organisations. I arranged these interviews through a mixture of cold calls to humanitarian organisations, snowball sampling outwards from interviewees, and connections through people I already knew working in the humanitarian system, until I reached saturation point with the interviews. To understand the secular, the faith-based must also be included in this research, as well as different levels of organisations from the international to the local. Some national organisations were also included because they work in partnership with international organisations and often represent a middleman between the international system and the local context. Likewise, the NGO staff sample included staff from an international background, as well as national, and local staff to ensure a range of perspectives were involved. The FGDs and interviews in the Philippines all happened within the time period of November 2014 to April 2015. Some interviews with staff then located outside the Philippines took place in the few months before and after this time period. In total, 264 people participated in the research.

Methodologically, the study underlines the socially constructed nature of different categories and the fluidity of positions in which people can hold supposedly contradictory beliefs at the same time. It is not for sociologists to affirm beliefs one way or another but instead to comprehend their social implications. The research aims in this way to uncover the complexity of secular-religious dynamics rather than to assign further rigid definitions. In the results, secular and faith-based organisations are broadly designated to give some indication of the background of the participants, while recognising that there are vast varieties of organisational identities within them, which are not discussed in detail here in order to maintain the anonymity of respondents and organisations. I have given some descriptors to orient the reader about different opinions, but I chose to anonymise all names and organisational names to allow respondents to speak freely about their critiques of the humanitarian system.

Reflexivity (the researcher's self-awareness of their own positionality and how that affects the research and its results) is highly important as it is a "major strategy for quality control in qualitative research" (Berger 2015, p. 219). I cannot ignore that it is my voice telling this story and you may wonder who I am in relation to this subject matter. My religious and geographical affiliations are the most pertinent questions. I feel comfortable in secular and religious environments. All my education and employment have been in secular environments and I grew up in the United Kingdom, one of the more secularised countries in the world. Having now lived in other contexts, I realise how I display elements of Eurocentric secularism in some ways. Yet I spent most of my youth highly involved in the Anglican Church and, in terms of religious tradition and cultural base, this is also a comfort zone. I have both been awed by religious beliefs and practices and disgusted by some of their manifestations in our world, likewise for secular beliefs and practices. Some might be dismayed by this fluid perspective; others may recognise themselves. I hope in my complete transparency about my own continuing journey and at times nebulous position that I can engage with you, as the reader, to approach the rest of this book as a constant dialogue between positions. As the secularity of Western academics (Fountain 2013a), as well as the Euro- and androcentrism of sociological theory (Alatas and Sinha 2017) and the Western nature of disaster research (Gaillard 2019), has been criticised, I am aware that I represent at least some elements of these categories and have been educated within these traditions. This book is an extended self-critique to some extent, as in the process of reflexivity one is bound to understand the faults of a Eurocentric secular position. As the research critiques a secular position it could be understood 1) by secularists to be from a religious person's critical view of the secular, 2) by religious believers as an indictment of the secular in order to support the faith-based. It is neither. I am not promoting a religious or secular viewpoint. I doubt that any one approach is the final answer and am more interested by the nuance in between.

Outline of chapters

The second chapter of the book makes the case for the classification of the humanitarian system as overarchingly secular in the power dynamics that contribute to the function of influential norms and dispositions at play. It takes a macro-level view of the international humanitarian system to understand the ways in which the emergent and non-linear aspects of secular-religious dynamics have evolved, based on historical insights into the place of the secular-religious dynamics in the growth of the humanitarian system, theoretical insights into the secular-religious dynamics of ethics, organisational typologies, and the humanitarian principles, and concludes with an overview of the main parameters of the norms of secularity in the humanitarian system.

The third and fourth chapters directly report on and analyse results from the humanitarian response to Typhoon Haiyan in the Philippines. In order to demonstrate the significance of religious beliefs and practices for disaster-affected people and ground the entwinement of religions and disasters as a necessary concept of analysis for humanitarian response, Chapter 3 uses a framework from classical theories of the sociology of religion to interrogate the aspects of religious beliefs and practices that were meaningful for people after Haiyan. The chapter also details the place of religions and disasters in the Philippines. Challenging some perspectives on religious beliefs and practices as fatalistic alone, the chapter explores how people can hold multiple, seemingly contradictory, perspectives together. A lack of awareness of these perspectives leads to missed opportunities for engagement and accountability to affected communities. The overarching argument of this chapter is that religious beliefs and practices strongly influence people's disaster experience, including their experience of humanitarian organisations, meaning that secular-religious dynamics are pertinent for understanding the positions of disaster-affected people.

The fourth chapter details the parameters of secularity in the humanitarian system as explained by humanitarians responding to Typhoon Haiyan. These secular humanitarian staff recount the intricacies of creating boundaries to define what is acceptable and unacceptable for the secular humanitarian system. Humanitarians defined secularity as no proselytising, a secular mission and vision for the organisation, religion as taboo, and respectfulness but also interestingly thought that secularity made them more impartial and effective, when results from affected people showed almost the exact opposite effects. The main argument in this chapter focuses on the idea that secular disassociation from religion is not a neutral stance, as many secular humanitarians expect, but has profound implications for the relevance and effectiveness of humanitarian assistance. It shows that secularity is a powerful force in the humanitarian system but is one of which most are unaware.

The fifth chapter contends with the question of a way forward for the humanitarian system, following on from the current gaps and problems uncovered in the previous chapters. I discuss humanitarian trends towards localisation and the intersection with secularity, as well as the trend towards religious engagement seen from various secular humanitarian actors. This chapter will both discuss theoretical elements, such as what can be learned from a post-secular approach for humanitarians, and real-world examples emanating from my experiences working on research into religion with secular humanitarian actors. The overall contention is that in the rush to look at religion and development, we have failed to properly see what needs to change in secular arenas, let alone in the fact that the humanitarian system is yet more secularised than the development sector. To bridge this, processes of (post-)secular reflexivity and religious literacy are suggested.

The final chapter summarises the main arguments of the book, concluding that secular-religious dynamics are influential in the humanitarian system, and that isolated secularity plays a role as a force of power and dominance, of differentiation and control. In order to establish balance and see processes such as localisation come to fruition, it will be necessary to deeply reconsider the current secular-religious dynamics at play in the humanitarian system.

Note

1 Wilson's descriptions (Wilson 2012, pp. 16–17) of these dichotomies are as follows: Institutional/ideational: "Religion's institutional element is observable and tangible and thus, easier to examine, in contrast to religion's ideational influences, which are more subtle, implicit and intangible."

Individual/communal: "religion exercises influence at an individual level or at a broader level. Again, I argue that religion's influence operates at both levels."

Irrational/rational: "aspects of religion can be consistent with liberal secular definitions of what is rational as well as displaying some 'irrational' characteristics."

Bibliography

Ager, A., and Ager, J., 2011. Faith and the Discourse of Secular Humanitarianism. *Journal of Refugee Studies*, 24 (3), 456–472.

Ager, A., and Ager, J., 2015. *Faith, Secularism, and Humanitarian Engagement: Finding the Place of Religion in the Support of Displaced Communities*. New York: Palgrave Macmillan.

Ager, J., Ager, A., and Abebe, B., 2014. Mental Health and Psychosocial Support in Humanitarian Emergencies in Africa: Challenges and Opportunities for Engaging with the Faith Sector. *Review of Faith and International Affairs*, 12 (1), 72–83.

Ager, J., Fiddian-Qasmiyeh, E., and Ager, A., 2015. Local Faith Communities and the Promotion of Resilience in Contexts of Humanitarian Crisis. *Journal of Refugee Studies*, 28 (2), 202–221.

Alatas, S.F., and Sinha, V., 2017. *Sociological Theory Beyond the Canon*. London: Palgrave Macmillan.

Aldridge, A., 2013. *Religion in the Contemporary World: A Sociological Introduction*. 3rd ed. Cambridge: Polity Press.

Asad, T., 1993. *Genealogies of Religion: Discipline and Reasons of Power in Christianity and Islam*. Baltimore and London: Johns Hopkins University Press.

Asad, T., 2003. *Formations of the Secular: Christianity, Islam, Modernity*. Stanford, Calif.: Stanford University Press.

Barder, O., and Talbot, T., 2016. *The World Humanitarian Summit: The System's Broken, Not Broke*. Washington DC: Center for Global Development.

Barnett, M., and Stein, J.G., 2012. Introduction: The Secularization and Sanctification of Humanitarianism. *In:* M. Barnett and J.G. Stein, eds. *Sacred Aid: Faith and Humanitarianism*. New York: Oxford University Press, Inc., 3–36.

Bennett, C., 2016. *Time to let go: Remaking Humanitarian Action for the Modern Era*. London: Humanitarian Policy Group, Overseas Development Institute.

Berger, P., 1999. The Desecularization of the World: A Global Overview. In: P.L. Berger, ed. *The Desecularization of the World: Resurgent Religion and World Politics*. Grand Rapids, MI: William B. Eerdmans Publishing Company, 1–18.

Berger, P., 2014. *The Many Altars of Modernity: Toward a Paradigm for Religion in a Pluralist Age*. Boston; Berlin: Walter de Grutyer GmbH & Co KG.

Berger, R., 2015. Now I See It, Now I Don't: Researcher's Position and Reflexivity in Qualitative Research. *Qualitative Research*, 15 (2), 219–234.

Browne, K.E., 2015. *Standing in the Need: Culture, Comfort, and Coming Home After Katrina*. Austin: University of Texas Press.

Browne, K.E., and Olson, L., 2019. *Building Cultures of Preparedness: A Report for the Emergency Management Higher Education Community*. Washingtion, DC: The U.S. Federal Emergency Management Agency (FEMA).

Bruce, S., 2011a. Defining Religion: A Practical Response. *International Review of Sociology/Revue Internationale de Sociologie*, 21 (1), 107–120.

Bruce, S., 2011b. *Secularization: In Defence of an Unfashionable Theory*. Oxford: Oxford University Press.

Burchardt, M., 2013. Faith-Based Humanitarianism: Organizational Change and Everyday Meanings in South Africa. *Sociology of Religion,* 74 (1), 30–55.

Bureau of Democracy, Human Rights and Labor, 2013. *International Religious Freedom Report for 2013: Philippines*. Washington, DC: U.S. Department of State.

Bush, R., Fountain, P.M., and Feener, R.M., 2015a. Introduction. *In: Religion and the Politics of Development*. London: Palgrave Macmillan, 1–9.

Bush, R., Fountain, P.M., and Feener, R.M., 2015b. Religious Actors in Disaster Relief: An Introduction – International Journal of Mass Emergencies and Disasters. *International Journal of Mass Emergencies and Disasters*, 33 (1), 1–16.

Cannon, T., Schipper, L., Bankoff, G., and Kruger, F., 2014. *World Disasters Report: Focus on Culture and Risk*. Geneva: International Federation of Red Cross and Red Crescent Societies.

Carden, D. and Clements, A.J., 2015. Coordinating the Response to Typhoon Haiyan. *Humanitarian Exchange Magazine*, Humanitarian Practice Network, no. 63 (January), 3–5.

Casanova, J., 2009. The Secular and Secularisms. *Social Research*, 76 (4), 1049–1066.

Casanova, J., 2019. *Global Religious and Secular Dynamics: The Modern System of Classification*. Leiden: Brill.

Clarke, G., and Jennings, M., eds., 2008. *Development, Civil Society and Faith-Based Organizations: Bridging the Sacred and the Secular*. Basingstoke: Palgrave Macmillan.

Clarke, M., and Halafoff, A., 2017. *Religion and Development in the Asia-Pacific: Sacred Places as Development Spaces*. Routledge, Abingdon and New York.

Collinson, S., and Elhawary, S., 2012. *Humanitarian Space: A Review of Trends and Issues*. London: Humanitarian Policy Group, Overseas Development Institute.

Curtis, H.D., 2018. *Holy Humanitarians, American Evangelicals and Global Aid*. Cambridge: Harvard University Press.

Davey, E., Borton, J., and Foley, M., 2013. *A History of the Humanitarian System: Western Origins and Foundations*. London: Overseas Development Institute (ODI).

Davies, C., 2010. *UK Medic May Have Been killed for Working with Christian Group* [online]. Available from: www.guardian.co.uk/world/2010/aug/08/uk-medic-afghan-murdered-christian-group.

Dodds, P., 2010. Haiti Earthquake Leads to Increased Tensions Among Religions [online]. *The Associated Press*. Available from: www.nola.com/religion/index. ssf/2010/02/haiti_earthquake_leads_to_increased_tensions_among_religions. html.

Donini, A., Fast, L., Hansen, G., Harris, S., Minear, L., Mowjee, T., and Wilder, A., 2008. *The State of the Humanitarian Enterprise*. Medford, MA: Feinstein International Center, Tufts University.

Eisenstadt, S.N., 2010. The Reconstruction of Religious Arenas in the Framework of 'Multiple Modernities.' In: B.S. Turner, ed. *Secularization*, Volume 1. London: SAGE Publications Ltd., 96–113.

Escandor, A., 2016. 3 Years After Typhoon Haiyan, Data Reveals Lessons in Funding and Rehabilitation [online]. *Devex*. Available from: www.devex.com/news/sponsored/3-years-after-typhoon-haiyan-data-reveals-lessons-in-funding-and-rehabilitation-88993 [Accessed 28 August 2019].

Ferris, E., 2005. Faith-based and Secular Humanitarian Organizations. *International Review of the Red Cross*, 87 (858), 311–325.

Fiddian-Qasmiyeh, E., 2011. The Pragmatics of Performance: Putting 'Faith' in Aid in the Sahrawi Refugee Camps. *Journal of Refugee Studies*, 24 (3), 533–547.

Fiddian-Qasmiyeh, E., and Ager, A., 2013. *Local Faith Communities and the Promotion of Resilience in Humanitarian Situations: A Scoping Study*. Oxford: Joint Learning Initiative on Faith and Local Communities and RSC Working Paper.

Field, J., 2017. What Is Appropriate And Relevant Assistance After a Disaster? Accounting for Culture(s) in the Response to Typhoon Haiyan/Yolanda. *International Journal of Disaster Risk Reduction*, 22, 335–344.

Financial Tracking Service, 2015. *Philippines – Typhoon Haiyan Strategic Response Plan* (November 2013 – October 2014) (Humanitarian response plan) [online].

FTS UNOCHA. Available from: https://fts.unocha.org/appeals/441/summary [Accessed 19 August 2015].

Fountain, P.M., 2013a. Toward a Post-Secular Anthropology. *The Australian Journal of Anthropology*, 24 (3), 310–328.

Fountain, P.M., 2013b. The Myth of Religious NGOs: Development Studies and the Return of Religion. *In:* G. Carbonnier, ed. *International Development Policy: Religion and Development*. Houndmills, Basingstoke, Hampshire; New York: Palgrave Macmillan.

Fountain, P.M., 2015. Proselytizing Development. In: E. Tomalin, ed. *The Routledge Handbook of Religions and Global Development*. Abingdon; New York: Routledge.

Fountain, P.M., Bush, R., and Feener, R.M., 2015. Religion and the Politics of Development. *In: Religion and the Politics of Development*. London: Palgrave Macmillan, 11–34.

Fox, J., 2001. Religion as an Overlooked Element of International Relations. *International Studies Review*, 3 (3), 53–73.

Freeman, D., 2019. *Tearfund and the Quest for Faith-Based Development*. Abingdon; New York: Routledge.

Gaillard, J.C., 2019. Disaster Studies Inside Out. *Disasters*, 43 (S1), S7–S17.

Geertz, C., 1993. Religion as a Cultural System. *In: The Interpretation of Cultures: Selected Essays*. London: Fontana Press, 87–125.

Ghandour, A.R., 2003. Humanitarianism, Islam and the West: Contest or Cooperation? *Humanitarian Exchange Magazine*, 25, *Humanitarian Practice Network*, 14–17.

Guha-Sapir, D., Below, R., and Hoyois, Ph., 2015. *EM-DAT: International Disaster Database – Country Profile – Philippines*. Brussels, Belgium: Université Catholique de Louvain.

Habermas, J., 2008. Notes on Post-Secular Society. *New Perspective Quarterly (NPQ)*, Fall, 17–29.

Hanley, T., Binas, R., Murray, J., and Tribunalo, B., 2014. *IASC Inter-agency Humanitarian Evaluation of the Typhoon Haiyan Response*. New York: UNOCHA, Inter-Agency Humanitarian Evaluation Steering Group.

Heffernan, T., Adkins, J., and Occhipinti, L., 2009. *Bridging the Gaps: Faith-based Organizations, Neoliberalism, and Development in Latin America and the Caribbean*. Lanham, MD: Lexington Books.

Hurd, E.S., 2007. *The Politics of Secularism in International Relations*. Princeton: Princeton University Press.

Joint Typhoon Warning Center, 2013. *Annual Tropical Cyclone Report 2013*. Pearl Harbour, Hawaii: Joint Typhoon Warning Center.

King, D.P., 2019. *God's Internationalists: World Vision and the Age of Evangelical Humanitarianism*. Philadelphia: University of Pennsylvania Press.

Knox Clarke, P., Stoddard, A., and Tuchel, L., 2018. *The State of the Humanitarian System 2018*. London: ALNAP.

Krüger, F., Bankoff, G., Cannon, T., Orlowski, B., and Schipper, E.L.F., eds., 2015. *Cultures and Disasters: Understanding Cultural Framings in Disaster Risk Reduction*. Abingdon: Routledge.

Lagmay, A.M.F., Agaton, R.P., Bahala, M.A.C., Briones, J.B.L.T., Cabacaba, K.M.C., Caro, C.V.C., Dasallas, L.L., Gonzalo, L.A.L., Ladiero, C.N., Lapidez, J.P., Mungcal, M.T.F., Puno, J.V.R., Ramos, M.M.A.C., Santiago, J., Suarez, J.K., and Tablazon, J.P., 2015. Devastating Storm Surges of Typhoon Haiyan. *International Journal of Disaster Risk Reduction*, 11, 1–12.

Lin, J.J., and Lin, W.I., 2016. Cultural Issues in Post-disaster Reconstruction: The Case of Typhoon Morakot in Taiwan. *Disasters*, 40 (4), 668–692.

Lincoln, B., 2006. *Holy Terrors: Thinking About Religion After September 11*. 2nd ed. Chicago, IL; London: University of Chicago Press.

Lynch, C., 2011. Religious Humanitarianism and the Global Politics of Secularism. *In:* C. Calhoun, M. Juergensmeyer, and J. Van Antwerpen, eds. *Rethinking Secularism*. Oxford; New York: Oxford University Press, Inc.

Mahmood, S., 2015. *Religious Difference in a Secular Age: A Minority Report*. Princeton: Princeton University Press.

Martin, D., 2010. Towards Eliminating the Concept of Secularization. In: B.S. Turner, ed. *Secularization*. London: SAGE Publications Ltd., 1–11.

Mavelli, L., and Petito, F., eds., 2014. *Towards a Postsecular International Politics: New Forms of Community, Identity, and Power*. Basingstoke, Hampshire: Palgrave Macmillan.

Merli, C., 2012. Religion and Disaster in Anthropological Research. *In:* M. Kearnes, F. Klauser, and S. Lane, eds. *Critical Risk Research*. Basingstoke: John Wiley & Sons, Ltd; Hampshire: Palgrave Macmillan., 43–58.

Mucke, P., 2013. *World Risk Report 2013*. Berlin: Bündnis Entwicklung Hilft (Alliance Development Works).

NEDA, 2013. *Reconstruction Assistance on Yolanda*. Pasig City, Philippines: National Economic and Development Authority (NEDA).

Ngo, M., 2018. *Between Humanitarianism and Evangelism in Faith-based Organisations: A Case from the African Migration Route*. Abingdon; New York: Routledge.

OCHA, 2013a. *Typhoon Haiyan, Situation Report No. 2 (as of 8 November 2013)*. Text.

OCHA, 2013b. *Philippines: Typhoon Haiyan Situation Report No. 22 (as of 10 December 2013)*. Text.

Ocon, G., and Neussner, O., 2015. Assessing Early Warning Efforts for Typhoon Haiyan in Leyte. *Humanitarian Exchange Magazine*, 63, 8–10.

Oliver-Smith, A., and Hoffman, S.M., 1999. *The Angry Earth: Disaster in Anthropological Perspective*. Psychology Press.

Paipais, V., 2018. Introduction: Political Theologies of the International – The Continued Relevance of Theology in International Relations. *Journal of International Relations and Development*, 1–9.

Patterson, O., Weil, F., and Patel, K., 2010. The Role of Community in Disaster Response: Conceptual Models. *Population Research and Policy Review*, 29 (2), 127–141.

Petersen, M.J., 2010. International Religious NGOs at the United Nations: A Study of a Group of Religious Organizations. *The Journal of Humanitarian Assistance*.

Redfield, P., 2012. Secular Humanitarianism and the Value of Life. In: C. Bender and A. Taves, eds. *What Matters? Ethnographies of Value in a Not So Secular Age*. New York: Columbia University Press, 144–178.

Rees, J.A., 2014. Religion in the Syntax of Power: A Postsecular Perspective on International Relations. *Politics, Religion & Ideology*, 15 (3), 456–472.

Riesebrodt, M., 2014. Religion in the Modern World: Between Secularization and Resurgence. *European University Institute*, Max Weber Programme (Max Weber Lecture No. 2014/01).

Seybolt, T.B., 2009. Harmonizing the Humanitarian Aid Network: Adaptive Change in a Complex System. *International Studies Quarterly*, 53 (4), 1027–1050.

Taylor, C., 2007. *A Secular Age*. Harvard: Harvard University Press.

Thaut, L.C., 2009. The Role of Faith in Christian Faith-Based Humanitarian Agencies: Constructing the Taxonomy. *Voluntas*, 20 (4), 319–350.

Thomas, S., 2005. *The Global Resurgence of Religion and the Transformation of International Relations: The Struggle for the Soul of the Twenty-first Century*. New York; Basingstoke: Palgrave Macmillan.

Tomalin, E., 2012. Thinking About Faith-Based Organisations in Development: Where Have We Got to and What Next? *Development in Practice*, 22, (5–6), 689–703.

Tomalin, E., 2013. In: R.M. Feener, P. Fountain, and R. Bush, eds. *Religion and the Politics of Development*. London: Routledge.

Tomalin, E., ed., 2015a. *The Routledge Handbook of Religions and Global Development*. Abingdon; New York: Routledge.

Tomalin, E., 2015b. Gender, Development, and the "De-privatisation" of Religion: Reframing Feminism and Religion in Asia. *In: Religion and the Politics of Development*. London: Palgrave Macmillan, 61–82.

Urquhart, A., and Tuchel, L., 2018. *Global Humanitarian Assistance Report 2018*. Bristol: Development Initiatives.

Walker, P., and Maxwell, D.G., 2008. *Shaping the Humanitarian World*. Abingdon; New York: Routledge.

Wilkinson, O., 2018a. When Local Faith Actors Meet Localisation. *Refugee Hosts*.

Wilkinson, O., 2018b. Secular Humanitarians and the Postsecular: Reflections on Habermas and the Typhoon Haiyan Disaster Response. *Journal of Contemporary Religion*, 33 (2), 193–208.

Wilson, E.K., 2012. *After Secularism: Rethinking Religion in Global Politics*. Basingstoke: Palgrave Macmillan.

Wilson, E.K., 2014. Faith-Based Organizations and Postsecularism in Contemporary International Relations. *In:* L. Mavelli and F. Petito, eds. *Towards a Postsecular International Politics: New Forms of Community, Identity, and Power*. Basingstoke, Hampshire: Palgrave Macmillan, 219–242.

Wilson, E.K., and Mavelli L., 2014. Faith and the Asylum Crisis: The Role of Religion in Responding to Displacement (Policy Paper). Groningen; Canterbury: University of Groningen; University of Kent. https://kar.kent.ac.uk/45313/.

Wilson, E.K., 2017. 'Power Differences' and 'the Power of Difference': The Dominance of Secularism as Ontological Injustice. *Globalizations*, 14 (7), 1076–1093.

Wisner, B., Blaikie, P.M., Cannon, T., and Davis, I., 2004. *At Risk: Natural Hazards, People's Vulnerability and Disasters*. London; New York: Routledge.

2 The secular humanitarian system

The humanitarian system, as an evolving, emerging, non-linear, and self-organising complex system, can be analysed through its historical evolution and then its current norms, such as the humanitarian principles, different styles of humanitarian ethics and reasoning, and the types of organisations within it. To identify the parameters of secularity and secular-religious dynamics in the humanitarian system, this chapter traces the defining elements of the secular humanitarian system, questioning whether there has been a secularisation process in the system, and how humanitarian ethics and humanitarian principles have defined boundaries that differentiate from secular and religious reasoning, serving to create the differentiation of faith-based organisations from secular organisations in the humanitarian system.

Secular-religious dynamics in the history of the humanitarian system

The humanitarian system, in its modern form, is a recent concept, dating only as far back as the nineteenth century in many accounts (Barnett 2011; Davey et al. 2013), if not much more recently. During this same period, debates around secularisation have sparked and continued and, as noted in Chapter 1, complete secularisation has been dismissed. Some have made the case that there is evidence of secularisation in the humanitarian system (Barnett 2011), but I would contend that the system demonstrates secular dominance in the current period coupled with secular-religious dynamics throughout its history. There was no one point at which the humanitarian system was only religious and no final point at which it is, or will be, totally secularised. Nevertheless, even a cursory glance at the history of humanitarian action demonstrates that secular-religious dynamics are at play and some secularising forces have influenced the shape of the current system. There has been secularity and religiosity involved since the earliest formations of humanitarianism. The very beginnings of the word 'humanitarian' are bound to early to mid-nineteenth century thinking from philosopher August Comte and others about a "humanitarian religion" or "Religion of Humanity" that grounded a view of humanity and helping others in scientific and non-theological positions, which called for altruism based on a "love of humanity" rather than divine motivation (Davies 2012, p. 3). Although still using the term "religion," these were decidedly secular (scientific, profane, removed from connection to divinity) conceptions of what is humanitarian. This conception of humanitarianism remains prevalent in contemporary humanitarian discourse in many ways, where "Humanitarianism is thus generally understood as an expression of the liberal ethos that humans ought to care for others irrespective of differences because of their universally shared humanity" (Gajaweera 2015, p. 108). I will further pick up on this in the section on humanitarian ethics in this chapter.

The periods of the humanitarian system are debated but broadly cover the mid-nineteenth century to the World Wars, the Cold War period, and the post-Cold War period until the present day (Barnett 2011; Davey *et al.* 2013). In this early age, Barnett sees many ties to religious influence but also the influence of secular Enlightenment thinking: "Enlightenment processes helped to translate sympathy into collective action . . . increasingly individuals organised into citizens' groups, associations, and committees to provide immediate relief and to agitate for greater public attention to the destitute and the vulnerable" (Barnett 2011, p. 51). Likewise, he cites evangelical movements leading to "an upsurge in social justice" (Barnett 2011, p. 53). The Abolitionist Movement, with its highly religious aspects, marks a moment in which the shape of humanitarian thoughts and endeavours begin to form as people came together to help others that were not in their own country. Humanitarians, in these early days, were driven by "forces of compassion, namely a Christian and civilizational mentality" (Barnett 2011, p. 56). From the very beginning, therefore, secular Enlightenment and religious perspectives are intermingled in the roots of the humanitarian system.

Religious thought affected the formation of one of modern humanitarianism's main secular players: the International Committee of the Red Cross (ICRC). Henri Dunant and the team he drew around him to start the ICRC in the later nineteenth century were Genevan Calvinists who aimed to "rescue soldiers and nourish Christian civilisation" by "stimulating Christian principles of charity and giving"(Barnett 2011, p. 78). On the other hand, Eglantyne Jebb, founder of the Save the Children in the early twentieth century, had more spiritual leanings, "which accommodated her belief in the oneness of the world and transcendental humanity" (Barnett 2011, p. 85). Both were operating on the basis of a transcendental concept of humanity, but from quite different perspectives. For Barnett, this marks the difference in humanitarianism in the nineteenth and twentieth centuries:

During the nineteenth century God and religion defined the transcendent for many (especially in the West). During the twentieth century a secularised humanity became more fashionable and more widely regarded as providing the transcendent foundations for an international community defined by considerable diversity.

(Barnett 2011, p. 103)

This switch places the oneness of humanity as the transcendent principle, following Comte, rather than divine transcendence. It is a process of secular and religious pluralisation in that the authority of religion is diversified as a range of secular and religious actors become involved. As motivation from a transcendent concept of humanity is still pinpointed as influential, this could be seen as the starting point of modern day contentions that humanitarianism is a type of secular faith (Benthall 2008; Barnett and Stein 2012; Paras and Stein 2012).

During and following the Second World War, as well as into the 1960s, the establishment of many existing humanitarian organisations takes place. Among these, there are secular and faith-based organisations. Some have initial religious ties but represented a mix of civil society actors and are now entirely secular, such as Concern Worldwide (Farmar 2002) and Oxfam (Oxfam 2019). Some FBOs were established but are very much part of the international secular humanitarian system, such as Catholic Relief Services, Catholic Agency for Overseas Development (CAFOD), and Christian Aid (Benthall 2017, p. 5). Others stand out for their adhesion to secular thought, such as Médecins Sans Frontières (MSF). Benthall argues that, as the modern aid system only dates back to the end of the Second World War and was largely secular ever since, it is the FBOs that have needed to adapt to secular aid from the beginning rather than vice versa (i.e., the secular NGOs secularising the aid system) (Benthall 2017, p. 4). Davey cites decolonisation in the 1960s as having a "profound effect on the development of NGOs" as "the skills, material and money wielded by Northern organisations were called upon to supplement those of the newly established Southern governments" (Davey 2013, p. 11). Jean Pictet's clarification of the ICRC's principles in 1965 began the process of standardisation across actors. The principles were established as the model to which one should adhere, although many of the concepts formalised by Pictet were not new to humanitarians. The 1960s represent a moment that could therefore be seen as the height of the secular humanitarian system – the definitive uncoupling from colonial mentalities related to religion and the standardisation of a secular humanitarian moral code. FBOs fitted into this structure rather than defined it.

One might think that this sounds like secularisation of the humanitarian system, but there is a missing puzzle piece (or indeed hundreds and thousands of pieces). Histories of humanitarianism have been particularly Western in their outlook and the organisations in the humanitarian system that are not from Western Europe have different conceptions of how secular and religious dynamics have influenced the system. Islamic conceptions of the global *umma* (Islamic community) have not been included in the debate. As Benthall points out, Islamic charities from Gulf states have been involved in conflict response for many years, many politically aligned and separate to Christian *or* secular universalisms that may try to make a claim to humanitarian "pretensions of an 'international community'" (Benthall 2017, p. 5). Likewise, interpretations of secularity and secularisation have been particularly Western in their outlook and related to an evolution of Judeo-Christian thought. Gajaweera argues that,

> it is important to specify how many of the ethical discourses, forms, and institutional processes that are assumed to be secular in the fields of humanitarianism and development – such as ideas of "empowerment," or the "sacralisation of life and the valorisation of suffering" found in the development and humanitarianism discourses – could also arguably be construed as Protestant in character.
>
> (Gajaweera 2015, p. 107)

Asad would be quick to remind us that definitions of the religious and the secular are not inventions of the West alone (Asad 1993) nor that the West obtains any level of pure political secularism, as opposed to misguided critiques of non-Western "others" who have "failed to embrace secularism and enter modernity" (Asad 2003, p. 10). Secularisation theories that posit religious resurgence around the world and the "de-privatisation" of religion (Casanova 1994) are shown to be only really of relevance to Western Europe (Casanova 2019, p. 33) because, as Tomalin puts it, "to talk about the 'de-privatisation' of religion in many settings makes little sense since religion was never 'privatised' in the first place, nor was it ever expected to become so" (Tomalin 2015, p. 64).

While the history of non-Western humanitarianisms is generally lacking, we can see that secular and religious dynamics have been relevant around the world (rather than the overly simplistic divide of secularisation in Europe and religions everywhere else). Mahmood explains that public-private divides are still significant in the ways in which secularity influences non-Western contexts (Mahmood 2015, p. 115). Breaking out of a Western lens, conceptions of secular-religious dynamics are less about defining abstract parameters around the religious and secular as modern outcomes of earlier Christian thought and more about understanding that it is "a misunderstood notion that the secular and the religious represent distinct domains of national life, leading to distinct subjectivities" (Huq 2012). Furthermore,

Mahmood implores us to remember that secularisation is "entwined with the history of power inequalities between the West and non-West, not least because many of its signature concepts, institutions, and practices were introduced through (direct or indirect) colonial rule" (Mahmood 2015, pp. 10–11), following Asad to assert that the Western or non-Western history is not the question, but an analysis of power related to the concepts of the secular and religious and "the forms of life that articulate them, the powers they release or disable" (Asad 2003, p. 17). Overall, therefore, we can assert that secular-religious dynamics will have been part of the dynamics of humanitarianism as part of the evolution of the system around the world, both as faith-based and secular actors are part of the system and as they are not part of the system as, for example, Benthall (2017) and Petersen (2016) have explained with some Muslim NGOs.

Ultimately, we must understand that any secularisation narrative in the humanitarian system will usually be only single-mindedly looking at Western histories. Secular NGOs founded in countries in the Global South have specific reasons for their secularity, commonly associated with the limits of civil society in their countries and the political ramifications of secular or religious organisational identity (Huq 2012). Likewise, this brief history has found that secular conceptions of the humanitarian have been present from the beginning of its history, with religious and secular narratives gaining and decreasing in prominence at certain times. This is not a story of linear secularisation, therefore, but a demonstration that secular and religious reasoning exist simultaneously, sometimes in parallel and sometimes intertwined to the point of very little distinction between the two. Nevertheless, Western European NGOs are within the bounds of much of secularisation theory, emanating from societies that have seen processes of decline in numbers, belief, and institutional differentiation. As such, the question is not whether secularisation has happened to the humanitarian system writ large, but how secularisation has affected Western European NGOs and related humanitarian institutions, such as EU donors, and then how these actors have asserted power and dominance in the humanitarian system to create a space in which secularity does have a forceful function. I will now explore the current state of the humanitarian system to interrogate secularity in the contemporary system.

The contemporary secular humanitarian system

Humanitarian ethics

Humanitarian ethics point towards some of the main denominational differences for secular humanitarians. Broadly speaking, the two ends of the spectrum for humanitarian ethics are those whose ethical reasoning is duty-based and those who are consequentialist, or goal-based. Duty-based reasoning regards the humanitarian action as the end in itself, rather than the means to an end. Taking a lead from the philosophy of Immanuel Kant, duty-based humanitarianism "means doing one's duty, and that duty requires being willing to help those in need" (Barnett and Weiss 2011, p. 112). Deontological ethics measures the goodness and rightness of the act, rather than its consequences. It is linked to the notion of a humanitarian imperative: that one must (or is duty-bound) to help when another is suffering. The problem with such ethical reasoning stems from the fact that many humanitarian actions, although they may seem good in themselves, such as delivering food to starving families, can have unforeseen repercussions, as was seen in Biafra (and many other cases since) when aid was co-opted by parties in the conflict for their own purposes (Davey 2013; Barnett 2011).

It was due to such instances that Mary B. Anderson used the alternative dictum of "Do No Harm," the mantra of a consequentialist style of ethical humanitarian reasoning, in which "the rightness of an action is determined by whether it helps to bring about a better outcome than its alternatives" (Barnett and Weiss 2011, p. 113). This more utilitarian type ethic helps to explain how organisations can justify leaving a suffering population in cases of instability where the position of speaking out against a corrupt regime, for example, is deemed necessary to save more in the long run than indirectly helping to the support the continuation of the regime by providing for suffering citizens. One of the problems with such reasoning is highlighted by Didier Fassin who pinpoints a hierarchy of consequences within contemporary humanitarian organisations in which there is a fundamental "ontological inequality underlying this transaction in human lives" (Fassin 2012, p. 226) between the more valued life of the Western humanitarian worker or soldier and the devalued life of the local staff member or members of the civilian population. It is a question of which consequence matters most. It might be the case for many organisations that it is more "right" for them to withdraw humanitarian workers and save their staff lives than it is to maintain a presence in an insecure region, even if there are thousands in need.

Fassin takes a particularly broad range of activities to be humanitarian, but very much focuses his definitions of humanitarian reason and government around the imperatives that drive us to act:

> humanitarian reason corresponds to this ultimate theological-political recess at the "points of weakness," where "the tragedy of the modern condition" can no longer be eluded. . . . I therefore propose that we consider humanitarian government as the response made by our societies to what is intolerable about the state of the contemporary world. . . . Thus humanitarian government has a salutary power for us because by

saving lives, it saves something of our ideas of ourselves, and because by relieving suffering, it also relieves the burden of this unequal world order.

(Fassin 2012, p. 252)

We are reminded that the faith-like elements of humanitarian action in our reaction to evil and suffering in our world creates a new theodicy (or a sociodicy as Fassin (2012, p. 181) puts it) that lets us believe once again that good can exist. This brings us back to the idea that humanitarian action should be judged upon acts alone. It is the intention behind the act that is humanitarian but, more than anything, secular humanitarian ethics revolves around the timeless question of suffering. One of the founders of MSF, Rony Braumann, defines the philosophy of humanitarianism around this point: "To the question, 'What is man?,' humanitarian philosophy replies simply, 'He is not made to suffer'" (Braumann 2002, 60 in Benthall 2017, p. 6). Reaching back to the very beginning of this chapter, we are reminded that "humanitarian religion" from Comte calls for a love of humanity and a focus on living to help others grounded in a scientific value of human life, rather than human dignity because we are created as the *imago dei*. The sociodicy created in secular humanitarian thought links the humanitarian imperative to alleviate suffering to the idea of humanitarians as the moral actors who can make good the problem of suffering in our world. We create evil and we are the answer to evil. We must be our own saviours. Just as Durkheim (1915) suggested that society is the soul of religion, that society itself is the "godhead" represented in religion, in secular humanitarian thought society is the soul of evil, the devil itself, and the sociodicy is that society, therefore, is the one that must answer to this evil and humanitarianism is one of the means through which to do this.

The fundamental reason why this is secular, even with conceptual links to formations of religious reasoning, is that everything is kept within the "real" world of society and our daily experiences of life, not a transcendent reality. Taylor (2007, pp. 19–20) describes a secular age as "one in which the eclipse of all goals beyond human flourishing becomes conceivable." This ties in with a conceptualisation of secular humanitarian action as that which prioritises saving and maintaining human life right now above all else – a type of "self-sufficing humanism" focused on the immediacy of human life. As Redfield puts it,

Any transcendence [humanitarianism] might claim would remain temporal and essentially attached to the figure of the human. Although at times their efforts might suggest something like a sacred value to life, the terms of evaluation are intrinsically medical: the relative health of bodies and well-being of minds remains unquestionably paramount, the only legitimate measures for relative success or failure.

(Redfield 2012)

Benthall echoes this, saying that humanitarian ideology is marked by "the importance granted to physical life as the supreme value, which is a major factor in contemporary morality with its foregrounding of compassion" (Benthall 2017, p. 8). To this extent, secular humanitarians have a moral and ethical structure distinct from religious reasoning. Secular humanitarianism is not beholden to religious interpretations, even as we recognise that these ethical constructs (deontological, consequentialist, sociodicy of suffering) have evolved, in part, from religious thought. They exist as ethical interpretations that do not rely on a notion of transcendent reality and are thoroughly based in and limited to worldly concerns about the physically bounded human life. Taylor defines one of the major characteristics of the secular conception of the person as the bounded and buffered self, separate from an enchanted life in which mystical, otherworldly forces have a part. This secular, bounded, and buffered person is "master of the meanings of things for it" (Taylor 2008). Its rationality is internally created and justified – it operates within the immanent frame, Taylor's terminology for the profane and physical world. Humanitarian ethics exists within this immanent frame.

Principles

The humanitarian principles are the next obvious avenue for consideration, worth considering in addition to overarching humanitarian ethics because of their high level of influence in the humanitarian system. Humanitarian actors commonly aim to abide by the "humanitarian principles" and, in turn, are defined by their adherence to the principles. This term refers to the defined set of principles that are believed to be core values for "correct" humanitarian action. Although the Red Cross define seven principles (Pictet 1979), four have become widely accepted. As defined by UN OCHA, they are:

- Humanity: Human suffering must be addressed wherever it is found. The purpose of humanitarian action is to protect life and health and ensure respect for human beings.
- Neutrality: Humanitarian actors must not take sides in hostilities or engage in controversies of a political, racial, religious or ideological nature.
- Impartiality: Humanitarian action must be carried out on the basis of need alone, giving priority to the most urgent cases of distress and

making no distinctions on the basis of nationality, race, gender, religious belief, class or political opinions.

• Independence: Humanitarian action must be autonomous from the political, economic, military or other objectives that any actor may hold with regard to areas where humanitarian action is being implemented.

(OCHA 2010)

While humanity is the principle in which one can most straightforwardly see equally religious and secular interpretations, neutrality and impartiality are the stickiest principles around which debate along secular and religious lines can start. As will be seen in Chapter 4, secular humanitarians particularly associate secularity with impartiality. Impartiality is here understood to represent two concepts: 1) that aid is distributed without discrimination on the basis of race, ethnicity, religion, gender, or otherwise, and 2) that aid is distributed based on need alone. Neutrality is non-affiliation with political and other associated parties that may have an agenda in the disaster response. I have had a Google Scholar Alert set up for many years now that notifies me when a new article discussing religion and humanitarianism comes out (I also have one for "secular" and "humanitarian," of course). By far the most frequent occurrence is this mention of impartiality. Much that is written on humanitarianism will mention religion once, but only once, and that will be to specify that humanitarian assistance is given without discrimination based on race, ethnicity, religion, or gender. It is a description that is ultimately one of the clearest designations of secular identity in humanitarianism, never mind the fact that humanitarian FBOs assiduously work to maintain strict impartiality as well (Lynch and Schwarz 2017, p. 639). This phrasing of impartiality underlines that religion is not part of principled humanitarian action and serves to distance humanitarian action from religious beliefs and practices in order to remain impartial. While gender has been mainstreamed as a large part of humanitarian thinking for many years, race, ethnicity, and religion remain under-theorised in relation to humanitarian action, considering that they can be so influential in the ways that communities react to disaster (Schipper 2015) and make up part of the intersectional aspects of the vulnerabilities that people face (Cannon *et al.* 2014). Scholars are also starting to note that elements such as race (Lynch 2019) and disability have not been sufficiently discussed (Kelman and Stough 2015) in international relations and disaster response. As Wilson puts it, this is to be expected of a secular approach:

> The influence of secular dualistic thinking on religion in IR is often evident in what scholars do not say about religion as much as what they do. Religion may be mentioned in parsing as a factor of influence,

along with other neglected cultural factors, such as ethnicity, and history, dismissed as irrelevant on the basis of it being institutional, individual and irrational, or simply not mentioned at all.

(Wilson 2012, p. 67)

Separating these aspects of life from the humanitarian principles creates a distancing in which religious belief and practice are not part of, or a separate and lesser part, the discourse. Ager and Ager (2015, p. 22) succinctly state that, "Formulaic secularism that seeks to separate religion from humanitarianism by exclusion is neither feasible nor appropriate in contexts where religion is intertwined with every element of public space." Ager and Ager (2015) pinpoint the presumptions of humanitarians that allow secularism to flourish within the system. First, that there is a "humanitarian presumption of modernity" and second a "humanitarian presumption of neutrality." The presumption of modernity echoes Wilson's observation that secularism is asserted in international relations through the "the exclusion of religion as part of progress and development . . . only undeveloped, pre-modern societies allow religion to influence politics and public life" (Wilson 2012, p. 24). Religion is irrational and modernity is rational meaning that religion must be excluded from public influence. Ager and Ager (2015, p. 15) specify that this puts an emphasis on the material in humanitarian response, noting "Rationalism . . . asserts the primacy of material causes," and adding that this leads to crises being conceptualised in terms of materials requiring technical responses alone. This is linked to secular humanitarian conceptions of "universal needs" that resolutely do not involve the spiritual but are grounded entirely in the physical (food, water, shelter). This ultimately leads to a paradox in the humanitarian system wherein there is a "strong presumption of progress towards modernity [that] clashes uncomfortably with the common mantra to 'respect local cultures and norms'" (Ager and Ager 2015, p. 15). In an analysis of Canadian and British donor strategies as regards to religion, Schroeder found that "the contemporary focus on result-based programming tends to breed an instrumentalist and technocratic approach to religion – aspects of religion that contribute to the attainment of development outcomes are valued, while other elements are dismissed as counter-developmental" (Schroeder 2016, p. 3). Although applied to development rather than humanitarianism, the same focus on results and bureaucracy provide the ideal environment for instrumentalisation of religion in secular humanitarianism as well. Just as we saw that humanitarian ethics is secular because it is tied to "self-sufficing humanism" (Taylor 2007, pp. 19–20) and removed from transcendent explanations, the secular presumption of modernity ties humanitarianism once again to that which is resolutely physical and immanent through a strong relation to materiality.

It has been argued since the early 1980s in development practice that basic needs should include religious elements (Wilber and Jameson 1980 in Tomalin 2013, p. 44), yet this has not trickled through to humanitarian conceptions of basic/universal needs.

Yet a secular outlook does not need to tie humanitarianism to the presumption of modernity and the materiality of need. A useful alternative posited by Eisenstadt is that of "multiple modernities." As he describes, "all 'modernising' societies developed distinct modern dynamics, distinctive ways of interpreting modernity, for which the original Western project constituted the crucial starting and continual – usually ambivalent – reference point but often went beyond it" (Eisenstadt 2010, p. 97). In this scenario, even a turn to fundamentalism, often interpreted as a return to the traditional, is understood as distinctly modern in its way. This approach gives balance to interpretations of what is happening outside of Western Europe by providing a way in which we can understand the secular-religious dynamics of other countries as something other than examples of backward societies in which secularisation has not yet arrived, but modern societies in which secular aspects play a part alongside the religious. This emphasises the relativity of the "functional secularism" of humanitarian action and the need for secular humanitarians to be aware of their " 'situatedness' – where they come from, and what their values are" (A. Ager in PHAP 2015, p. 12). Mahmood has critiqued this approach, saying that secularism is not expressed in a "plurality of local cultural forms. . . . Rather . . . [it] takes strikingly similar forms across geographic contexts" (Mahmood 2015, p. 10). Even while secularism is displayed in many ways around the world, the notion of "multiple modernities" nevertheless encourages someone with a secular worldview to break out of a paternalistic mindset related to secularity, if they hold such a bias.

The presumption of neutrality, meanwhile, refers to humanitarian actors avoiding "association with groups that could be represented as suggesting alignment with their views with respect to politics, race, religion or ideology" (Ager and Ager 2015, p. 18). This translates into secular humanitarian actors being sensitive to being seen to engage with religious actors and a presumption that secularity in an organisation ensures neutrality. In turn, this leads to the privatisation of religion from the humanitarian public space, even when religion plays an influential public role globally. The principles do not always help humanitarians because, in one respect, they encourage disengagement with religious issues in a humanitarian context (Ager and Ager 2015, pp. 5, 90; Ager 2014) where they may be deeply influential and a necessary aspect of the dynamics in that context, both in terms of the other local actors working on the response and the dynamics of vulnerability and risk that contribute to disaster impacts for the affected people. Although these principles are in place to protect humanitarian space and equally the rights of people humanitarians serve, there are some suggestions that an absolute reliance on these principles may do more harm than good in some scenarios in relation to religion. Ager and Ager (2015, p. 64) sum up this struggle, saying, "It is a curious distortion of this laudable goal [neutrality] that local agendas and forms of thinking are displaced to the margins, while Western, secular constructions of religion enjoy relatively unchallenged power."

The effect on FBOs of the secularity of these principles has been to enforce strict delineations about the place of religion. In Lebanon, Salek reports that questions about the humanitarian principles posed to Islamic Relief staff and partner organisations were "met with strong pronouncements on the importance of non-discrimination, with any discussion of faith being first understood in terms of its potential risk to humanitarian principles" (Salek 2015, p. 364). I have also met with this response in interviews with faith-based actors, both international and national, in interviews in the Philippines, South Sudan, and Nigeria. They rush to affirm that, above all, they uphold non-discrimination and never bias humanitarian assistance on religious grounds. While affirming that this is largely a positive that allows for fairly distributed assistance, when looking specifically at the effects of secularity in the humanitarian system we see that this is one of the most clearly communicated "rules" that is understood and implemented around the world as a marker of acceptability in the humanitarian system. Yet, in fact, there have been reports that the reputation of local religious actors in the eyes of local populations have been tarnished by their involvement with secular INGOs (Ivarsson Holgersson 2013) because of the biases present within a particularly secular worldview, meaning that the secular presumption of neutrality and impartiality makes the humanitarian system more partial. Instituted as secular principles, the humanitarian principles are removed from the realms of religious reasoning, without an understanding that the enforced secularity of these principles in themselves is an act of differentiation and, thus, discrimination towards other world views and the possibility for shared understandings. As former Deputy High Commissioner for Refugees Alexander Aleinikoff stated, "a secular humanitarianism is partial because faith means a lot to people and one cannot not take faith into account" (Ager and Ager 2015, p. 19). While the international system might abide by a secular standard, Walsh reminds us "It is virtually impossible to imagine global citizenship without recognising that the vast majority of such citizens are believers who do not view their beliefs as quaint curiosities" (Walsh 2012, p. 57).

The way in which the principles are communicated and enforced has made any but the strictest interpretation feel unwelcome and dangerous, particularly for FBOs in their quest to maintain legitimacy in the secular humanitarian sphere. As Salek continues, "In the humanitarian sector, "impartiality" and "neutrality" seem to have led to silence on religious discourse, their commonalities being missed where discussion on shared values is avoided rather than integrated into discussion on the principles of humanitarian action. This further solidifies secular and religious distinctions in the humanitarian system, as Gajaweera describes,

> A dominant understanding of what has been called "secular humanitarianism" is that it is founded on a cosmopolitan ethic based on liberal Enlightenment values that are motivated by principles such as human equality, individual rights, and reason. "Faith-based humanitarianism," on the other hand, is often regarded as an ethic of care founded on religious principles of belief, spiritual motivation, and the sacred.
>
> (Heffernan 2007 in Gajaweera 2015, pp. 106–107)

This opens up the debate that secular organisations are more neutral in comparison to supposedly religiously partial FBOs. Ager and Ager (2015, p. 5) sum this up as a "working consensus" that has emerged in humanitarian action, although never explicitly stated, in which

> Religion, given its potential divisiveness, alignment to violence and intolerance, and its belonging to the realm of "ultimate ideals," is not an appropriate domain for humanitarian engagement. In order to "enjoy the confidence of all," agencies need to operate above the fray of religious ideology and practice, consigning religion's protected free exercise to the private sphere.

Religious humanitarianism sparks images of proselytisation and manipulation, even though some authors have posited that it is "donor proselytism" rather than religious proselytism that is the most powerful and divisive force at play in the humanitarian system (Lynch and Schwarz 2017). The Red Cross Code of Conduct is equally a principle setting document in the humanitarian system and it "engages in explicit boundary policing" (Fountain 2015, p. 82), defining in its third point that "Aid will not be used to further a particular political or religious standpoint" (ICRC 1994). Fountain points out, however, this supposedly simple point has "frayed edges" in that much humanitarian assistance has been politicised and the Code of Conduct also has to affirm that FBOs are free to espouse religious positions, according to the Universal Declaration of Human Rights (Fountain 2015, p. 82).

While asserting the importance of neutrality and impartiality, a more religiously literate *and* culturally sensitive approach would be to ask for the commonalities and similar interpretations from context-specific principles around aid, a process that does not happen frequently enough but has been advocated for and described by others, such as Engeland (2016) who seeks to learn from the "Muslim legal instrument of *maslaha*, which protects the public interest" without reverting into complete cultural relativism. Having said that, cultural context, including religious interpretation, is not the biggest threat to the humanitarian principles. This focus on threats to the principles should be understood within the broader debate around new humanitarianism and the evolution of the principles. There are those within the humanitarian sphere who would see a stark contrast between organisations who are more pragmatic and those who strictly adhere to the principles (Barnett 2012, p. 195). In the post-9/11 global environment in which it is perceived that humanitarian space has shrunk (Collinson and Elhawary 2012), the principles have once again come to the fore in international debate with political instrumentalisation seen as the biggest threat to principled humanitarian action.

Typologies of organisations

Yet FBOs also adhere to these ethics and principles and align them with religious interpretations. Secular humanitarian ethics are not exclusive to secular humanitarians. Turning to typologies of organisations instead, we see that FBOs are often set apart and this may help further pinpoint what makes secular humanitarian reasoning distinct. Taylor *et al.* (2012, p. 16) give a breakdown of those actors that might be present in the humanitarian system as a whole, which are the INGOs and National NGOs (NNGOs), UN agencies, the International Movement of the Red Cross/Red Crescent, host governments, regional intergovernmental organisations, donor government agencies, and then add that there are

> non-core humanitarian actors that work in parallel and often in coordination with the rest of the humanitarian system – but which have different ultimate goals and approaches – includ[ing]: militaries; private-sector entities, including commercial contractors; religious institutions (differentiated from faith-based operational aid organisations); diaspora groups and formal and informal private givers.

The 2018 update of this report reaffirms a similar line, saying "civil society groups (such as faith groups) that do not have an explicitly humanitarian function" (Knox Clarke *et al.* 2018, p. 32). Note that these authors, indirectly summarising the secular humanitarian system, include FBOs within the grouping of other aid organisations by differentiation or negation. FBOs are not religious institutions for these authors, as those are defined separately, and they are, therefore, in line with the "ultimate goals and approaches" of other INGOs. There is an institutional differentiation affirmed as part of the humanitarian system – religious institutions are *not* core humanitarian actors – but FBOs are counterparts and accepted as long as they follow the rules of the secular humanitarian system. It is this deceptively throwaway term, "ultimate goals and approaches," that marks religious institutions as separate and FBOs as having, I would argue, accepted secular humanitarian goals and approaches, making them part of the system.

Even within the INGOs there are a range of types of organisations that can be broadly categorised according to their mission and values. Stoddard defines organisations as falling into the categories of Wilsonian ("more dependent on and cooperative with governments, short time horizon, and a service delivery emphasis") or Dunantist ("more independent of and oppositional towards government, long time horizon, advocacy emphasis") (Stoddard 2003, p. 3) to explain some of the differences between organisations. The history of the difference between the principled and independent approach of ICRC founder, Henri Dunant, and the values of Woodrow Wilson, "who hoped to project US values and influence as a force for good in the world," (Stoddard 2003, p. 2) explains the divide. Stoddard explicitly states that this refers to secular NGOs, which immediately poses the question as to what happens with the FBOs working in similar areas. Many US FBOs receive substantial funding from the US government (Center for Faith and the Common Good 2017). US funding is secular, due to the Establishment Clause of the US Constitution, but the United States Agency for International Development's (USAID's) rules allow for any FBO to be funded and even to continue religious activities as long as they remain completely separate from the time and location of the USAID funded activities,[1] demonstrating the US' complex relationship around political secularism. The Dunantist approach is also secular in its strict adherence to the humanitarian principles, yet there are also FBOs that are deeply critical of governments, receive the large part of their funding from non-government sources, thanks to religious tithing (Hopgood and Vinjamuri 2012; Center for Faith and the Common Good 2017), and are activist in their emphasis on speaking out on ethical issues in humanitarian contexts.

The strict Dunantist approach could be seen as a secular faith in itself. In line with Benthall's cornucopia model (Benthall 2008, p. 62) we can see that almost all types of organisation can be seen to have some religious elements and lie on a spectrum from the weak to the strong religious field. However, this should not be confused with secular organisations being faith-based. While advocating a continuum approach for recognising where an organisation lies on a scale from the religious to the secular, the level of consciousness in which secular humanitarians participate in religious-like behaviour must be involved in any analysis. Do the humanitarians intend to act like a religious martyr or participate in religious-like ritual, as Benthall suggests are signs of religious elements for MSF, for example? It must be underlined that humanitarianism is only ever described as a *secular* faith. As I have argued elsewhere, we must be careful when we use terms that describe the principled humanitarian approach as "sacred" as it is not a theologically, transcendentally understood version of the sacred, but a description of the principled approach as *really, really* important to our conception of contemporary humanitarianism. This means that "a generalised statement about humanitarianism as a secular faith undermines the role of religious faith in humanitarian action" (Wilkinson 2014). As opposed to Barnett and Stein's ideas of the sanctification of secular humanitarian action (as well as the secularisation of religious humanitarian action), I see that this sanctification is not as seriously persuasive and powerful and it is the secular in the humanitarian system that remains the most influential. While Barnett and Stein's approach was useful in the first debates around this subject to open the space to see co-constitutive secular and religious dynamics (rather than starkly separate religious and secular approaches), the debate can now move on about how these dynamics play out. There is a sufficient amount of nuance in the secular-religious dynamics of humanitarianism that describing humanitarianism as a secular faith is an over-essentialisation that loses important analyses of power and privilege.

Dunantist approaches are also purist in their formulation of humanitarianism. Benthall explains the effects of "puripetal force" as he terms it, i.e., the push towards purity. Rather than seeking to define secular and religious boundaries, he sees how different types of purity influence the ways in which humanitarian organisations work. Building on Petersen's conceptions of "secularising Islam" and "sacralising aid" (Petersen 2016, pp. 12–13), he defines how organisations like Islamic Relief Worldwide (based in the UK) have "achieved an astute, if sometimes contentious, balance between the two purisms of Islam and humanitarianism, but with a leaning toward the latter" (Benthall 2016, p. 38), whereas organisations such as the International Islamic Relief Organisation and the World Assembly of Muslim Youth (based in Saudi Arabia) seek to preserve Muslim identity and give "de facto preference in allocation of its resources to Muslim populations" (Benthall 2016, p. 41). Strictly Dunantist humanitarianism, such as that of ICRC, is then equally classified as a quest for purity. Without using the terms secular and religious, Benthall nevertheless sets up two spheres of puripetal force – humanitarianism and Islam with Dunantist and Salafi interpretations representing the quests for the purest form of each. Organisations like Islamic Relief Worldwide represent a bridging between humanitarian and religious worlds.

From secularisation theory, the categorisation of organisational typologies along secular and religious lines also ties in with the process of institutional differentiation in which religious institutions do not hold ultimate power and prestige and instead secular institutions are dominant and agenda setting. This does not happen to the extent that religious institutions no longer exist in the case of the humanitarian system (i.e., not complete secularisation), but to the extent that the FBOs are separate and must make a claim to legitimacy rather than have it as default. Riesebrodt argues that this can be an advantage in some ways, saying "Religious institutions can create their own public sphere and participate in general public discourses. One could even argue that because of social differentiation, religion gains in autonomy and legitimacy to critique these other spheres" (Riesebrodt 2014, p. 3). While speaking of social differentiation in societies at large, it is applicable to the humanitarian system as we see a growing recognition of FBOs' perspectives (Bush *et al.* 2015, p. 5) and legitimacy of many faith-based humanitarian organisations in the secular humanitarian system. Secularity in the humanitarian system is not mutually exclusive to strong legitimacy, just not dominant authority, for FBOs therefore.

Applying these thoughts from an investigation of humanitarian typologies, organisations from non-Western settings have their own methods of understanding and dealing with secularity in the humanitarian system. In an example of a Japanese NGO (Organisation for Industrial, Spiritual and Cultural Advancement – OISCA) working in Myanmar, Watanabe purposefully chooses to remain distant from the idea of the secular, instead preferring the term "nonreligion":

> While OISCA aid workers adhere to the Japanese state's injunction to maintain religion in its proper place by claiming that they are not a religious organisation, their claim to be nonreligious and their appeal to a Shinto ecological worldview is not about liberal subjectivities. Thus, to use the term "secular" would be misleading. . . . Although OISCA staffers were also engaged in boundary-making practices, these actions involved a distancing from both categories rather than a claim of one over the other. . . . Their aim was to change the terms of engagement. The word "nonreligious," which includes the term "religious" in its negation, is an attempt at capturing the ambiguous position that OISCA staffers sought to create.
>
> (Watanabe 2015, p. 227)

Reaffirming that there is not an either/or between secular and faith-based organisations, this conceptualisation of nonreligion for OISCA goes one step further in that they are removed even from a spectrum of religious to secular states of organisational identity. Gajaweera, additionally and somewhat countering Watanabe's distancing from the secular, explains how an NGO in Sri Lanka formed a Buddhist cosmopolitan ethic, which allowed alignment with secular humanitarianism in order to "project an image of the organisation as squarely within the project of secular modernisation for the purposes of appealing to the international community" (Gajaweera 2015, p. 117), suggesting that

> it is a particular kind of cosmopolitan ethic that NGO workers, donors, and volunteers actively produced in order to strategically enact a humanitarian universality that transcends geographical and social distance. These entanglements produce what David McMahan (2008) described as a "transnational genre of Buddhism" that could be practiced even in what we conceive as consisting of a secularised context.
>
> (Gajaweera 2015, p. 123)

Mahmood and Asad's injunctions from Chapter 1 to follow the *power* of secular and religious categorisations pushes us to see that the organisational identity of these NGOs was shaped in relation to the dominant power in the arena in which they sought to have a place – for the Buddhist NGO in Sri Lanka this was in the secular international humanitarian system following the tsunami, while for OISCA this was in relation to the Japanese government and the formations of secular and non-secular identity in Japanese society. Overall, examining typologies and organisational identities has demonstrated the secularity of the humanitarian system in the differentiation between secular and faith-based actors and the need for non-secular actors to fit into the secular system. Yet the secularity of the system is not absolute and there is space for legitimacy and reinterpretation of views that do not confine to secular bounds alone.

Conclusion: the humanitarian system's secular parameters

From ethics, principles, typologies, and the evolution of the humanitarian system, can we find any overarching characteristics of secularity? The effects of secularising forces on academics and practitioners have been summarised as the assumption of

> the natural evolution toward a universal morality that transcends the need for metaphysical moorings . . . a commendable side effect of

democratisation and modernisation, and . . . the result of the globalisation of a modern state system in which religion has been privatised
once and for all.

(Hurd 2012, p. 45)

Jones and Petersen (2011, p. 1291) characterise the engagement of religion
in development as instrumental ("it is interested in understanding how religion can be used to do development 'better'"), narrow ("a narrow focus
on faith-based organisations, which is in many consequence of the need to
understand religion instrumentally"), and normative ("based on normative
assumptions in terms of how both religion development are conceptualised:
religion is understood to be apart 'mainstream' development, while development is defined as that thing development agencies do"). Ager and Ager
elaborate further on the contention that the impacts of secularity are pervasive in the international humanitarian system, explaining that, in line with
secularisation theories, the religious in humanitarianism has been banished
to the private sphere. The effect of secularity on the international humanitarian system "is primarily focused on controlling religion and limiting its
public power" (Ager and Ager 2015). Thus the "public sphere" of the system is secularised. Ultimately, they find that functional secularism has three
effects on religion in humanitarian action (Ager and Ager 2015, p. 12):

1   Privatisation: "Religion is not necessarily discounted, but its dynamics
    and challenges are seen to belong to the private worlds of believers
    and/or adherents, which have no legitimacy within public space."
2   Marginalisation: "The secular script . . . does not merely contain reli-
    gion; it disempowers it by pushing it to the margins of consideration."
3   Instrumentalisation: "Reflecting a Weberian approach, religion is
    assessed in terms of its benefit or detriment to predetermined goals. . . .
    Instrumentalisation recognises the resources that are available through
    local faith communities and seeks to co-opt these for non-religious
    purposes."

These three effects mean that religion exists peripherally within the secular
humanitarian consciousness as it is unavoidable in most contexts, but that
it has been taken out of humanitarian discourse (it is not seen as a relevant
or appropriate topic of discussion), relegated to private lives alone (for both
beneficiaries and staff), and only recognised when it can be of use to a secular humanitarian agenda (e.g., when religion can provide further funding
through local level or international financing mechanisms, see discussions
on Islamic zakat for a recent, wide-reaching example (Stirk 2015)).
    These are summaries from others about the salient aspects of secular-
ity on international relations, religion and development, and religion and

humanitarianism, much aligned with what we have seen in the humanitarian system in this chapter. From the review presented in this chapter, we have seen how the idea of the oneness of humanity as the transcendent concept of humanitarian ethics has been part of the humanitarian system from the beginning and is decidedly secular, as well as the emptying of humanitarian goals from religious understanding (e.g., the absence of spiritual support in psychosocial response). We have seen how the humanitarian system has a "presumption of modernity" inherent in the focus on technical and material aspects of life. We have seen how religion is distanced and privatised from the secular humanitarian public sphere, often using the humanitarian principles as justification for this distancing. Following Scott Thomas' "Westphalian Presumption" of the privatisation and marginalisation of religion in international society (Wilson 2012, p. 48), religion is privatised and marginalised in the international society that constitutes the humanitarian system. We have seen how the humanitarian system is instrumentalising and uses the dominance of secularity to create an environment in which religious reasoning must fit within secular standards. Overall, secularity in the humanitarian system is summarised as a belief in the oneness of humanity in this world (as separate from divinely created human oneness) and morality created within the immanent frame of this world, an understanding of modernity in that modern ways of operating will focus on the technical and material, the marginalisation and privatisation of religion to the extent that the secular is the default, and the ability to wield secularity as a part of humanitarian power dynamics, including the ability to instrumentalise religions.

Note

1 "USAID 'Rule' for Participation by Religious Organisations: The Rule generally ensures that faith-based and community organisations are able to compete fairly for USAID funding, and that USAID programming decisions are based on the program eligibility criteria, without regard to the religious character or affiliation of applicants. Moreover, although faith-based organisations may not use direct USAID funds for explicitly religious activities, including activities that involve overt religious content such as worship, religious instruction, or proselytisation, they may continue to engage in religious activities as long as they are separate in time or location from the programs or services funded with direct financial assistance from USAID, and participation must be voluntary for beneficiaries of the programs or services funded with such assistance." www.usaid.gov/faith-and-opportunity-initiatives/usaid-rule-participation

Bibliography

Ager, A., 2014. Faith and Secular: Tensions in Realising Humanitarian Principles. *Forced Migration Review* 48 (November): 16–18.

Ager, A., and Ager J., 2015. *Faith, Secularism, and Humanitarian Engagement: Finding the Place of Religion in the Support of Displaced Communities*. New York: Palgrave Macmillan.

Asad, T., 1993. *Genealogies of Religion: Discipline and Reasons of Power in Christianity and Islam.* Baltimore; London: Johns Hopkins University Press.

Asad, T., 2003. *Formations of the Secular: Christianity, Islam, modernity.* Stanford, CA: Stanford University Press.

Barnett, M., 2011. *Empire of Humanity: A History of Humanitarianism.* Ithaca, NY: Cornell University Press.

Barnett, M., and Stein, J.G., 2012. Introduction: The Secularization and Sanctification of Humanitarianism. *In:* M. Barnett and J.G. Stein, eds. *Sacred Aid: Faith and Humanitarianism.* New York: Oxford University Press, Inc., 3–36.

Barnett, M., and Weiss, T., 2011. *Humanitarianism Contested: Where Angels Fear to Tread.* London: Routledge.

Barnett, Michael. 2012a. "Faith in the Machine? Humanitarianism in an Age of Bureaucratization." In *Sacred Aid: Faith and Humanitarianism*, edited by Janice Gross Stein and Michael Barnett, 188–210. New York: Oxford University Press, Inc.

Benthall, J., 2008. *Returning to Religion: Why a Secular Age is Haunted by Faith.* London: I.B. Tauris & Co Ltd.

Benthall, J., 2016. Puripetal Force in the Charitable Field. *Asian Ethnology*, 75 (1), 29–51.

Benthall, J., 2017. Humanitarianism as Ideology and Practice. *In: The International Encyclopedia of Anthropology.* American Cancer Society, 1–9.

Bush, R., Fountain, P., and Feener, R.M., 2015. Introduction. *In: Religion and the Politics of Development.* London: Palgrave Macmillan, 1–9.

Cannon, T., Schipper, L., Bankoff, G., and Kruger, F., 2014. *World Disasters Report: Focus on Culture and Risk.* Geneva: International Federation of Red Cross and Red Crescent Societies.

Casanova, J., 1994. *Public Religions in the Modern World.* 1st ed. Chicago: University of Chicago Press.

Casanova, J., 2019. *Global Religious and Secular Dynamics: The Modern System of Classification.* Brill.

Center for Faith and the Common Good, 2017. *Sources of Revenue and International Expenditures of US Faith-Based NGOs, Based on IRS 990 Forms for Fiscal Years 2011–2015* [online]. Available from: www.faithforcommongood. org/uploads/4/8/4/9/48493789/updated_sources_of_revenue_and_international_ expenditures_of_us_faith-based_ngos_fy2011-15.pdf [Accessed 26 August 2019].

Collinson, S., and S. Elhawary. 2012. *Humanitarian Space: A Review of Trends and Issues.* London: Humanitarian Policy Group, Overseas Development Institute.

Davey, E., Borton, J., and Foley, M., 2013. *A History of the Humanitarian System: Western Origins and Foundations.* London: Overseas Development Institute (ODI).

Davies, K., 2012. *Continuity, Change and Contest: Meanings of 'Humanitarian' from the 'Religion of Humanity' to the Kosovo war.* London: ODI Humanitarian Policy Group.

Durkheim, E., 1915. *The Elementary Forms of the Religious Life.* London: George Allen & Unwin Ltd.

Eisenstadt, S.N., 2010. The Reconstruction of Religious Arenas in the Framework of 'Multiple Modernities.' *In: Secularization*, Volume 1. London: SAGE Publications Ltd., 96–113.

Engeland, A.V., 2016. Contextualisation of Humanitarian Assistance and its Shortcomings in International Human Rights Law. *Israel Law Review*, 49 (2), 169–195.

Farmar, T., 2002. *Believing in Action: The First Thirty Years of Concern 1968–1998*. Dublin: A. & A. Farmar.

Fassin, D., 2012. *Humanitarian Reason: A Moral History of the Present Times*. Berkeley, CA; London: University of California Press.

Fountain, P.M., 2015. Proselytizing Development. *In: The Routledge Handbook of Religions and Global Development*. Abingdon; New York: Routledge.

Gajaweera, N., 2015. Buddhist Cosmopolitan Ethics and Transnational Secular Humanitarianism in Sri Lanka. *In: Religion and the Politics of Development*. London: Palgrave Macmillan, 105–128.

Hopgood, S., and Vinjamuri, L., 2012. Faith in Markets. *In:* J.G. Stein, ed. *Sacred Aid: Faith and Humanitarianism*. New York: Oxford University Press, Inc., 38–64.

Huq, Samia. 2012. "Secularism and the Freedom to Transform Lives." *The Immanent Frame* (blog). May 3, 2012. https://tif.ssrc.org/2012/05/03/secularism-and-the-freedom-to-transform-lives/.

Hurd, E.S., 2012. The Politics of Secularism. *In:* A. Stepan and M.D. Toft, eds. *Rethinking Religion and World Affairs*. New York: Oxford University Press, Inc., 36–54.

ICRC, 1994. *Code of Conduct for the International Red Cross and Red Crescent Movement and Non-Governmental Organizations (NGOs) in Disaster Relief*. Geneva: ICRC, 1.

Ivarsson Holgersson, C., 2013. The Give and Take of Disaster Aid: Social and Moral Transformation in the Wake of the Tsunami in Sri Lanka. PhD Thesis. Gothenburg: University of Gothenburg, School of Social Studies. http://hdl.handle.net/2077/33687.

Jones, B., and Petersen, M.J., 2011. Instrumental, Narrow, Normative? Reviewing Recent Work on Religion and Development. *Third World Quarterly*, 32 (7), 1291–1306.

Kelman, I., and Stough, L.M., 2015. (Dis)Ability and (Dis)Aster. *In:* I. Kelman and L.M. Stough, eds. *Disability and Disaster: Explorations and Exchanges*. London: Palgrave Macmillan, 3–14.

Knox Clarke, P., Stoddard, A., and Tuchel, L., 2018. *The State of the Humanitarian System 2018*. London: ALNAP, Full Report.

Lynch, C., 2019. The Moral Aporia of Race in International Relations. *International Relations*, 33 (2), 267–285.

Lynch, C., and Schwarz, T., 2017. Humanitarianism's Proselytism Problem. *International Studies Quarterly*, 60 (4).

Mahmood, S., 2015. *Religious Difference in a Secular Age: A Minority Report*. Princeton: Princeton University Press.

OCHA, 2010. OCHA on Message: *Humanitarian Principles*. Available from: www.ochanet.unocha.org.

Oxfam, 2019. Oxfam's History [online]. *Oxfam America*. Available from: www.oxfamamerica.org/explore/about-oxfam/our-history/ [Accessed 7 August 2019].

Paras, A., and Stein, J.G., 2012. Bridging the Sacred and the Profane in Humanitarian Life. *In: Sacred Aid: Faith and Humanitarianism*. New York: Oxford University Press, Inc.

Petersen, M.J., 2016. *For Humanity or for the Umma?: Aid and Islam in Transnational Muslim NGOs*. Oxford: Oxford University Press.

PHAP, 2015. *Live Online Consultation: Faith and Religion in Humanitarian Action*. Geneva: Professionals in Humanitarian Assistance and Protection and World Humanitarian Summit.

Pictet, J., 1979. *The Fundamental Principles of the Red Cross: Commentary*. International Federation of Red Cross and Red Crescent Societies.

Redfield, P., 2012. Secular Humanitarianism and the Value of Life. *In: What Matters? Ethnographies of Value in a not so Secular Age*. New York: Columbia University Press, 144–178.

Riesebrodt, M., 2014. Religion in the Modern World: Between Secularization and Resurgence. *European University Institute*, Max Weber Programme (Max Weber Lecture No. 2014/01).

Salek, L.V., 2015. Faith Inspiration in a Secular World: An Islamic Perspective on Humanitarian Principles. *International Review of the Red Cross*. Cambridge, 97 (897–898), 345–370.

Schipper, E.L.F., 2015. Religion and Belief Systems: Drivers of Vulnerability, Entry Points for Resilience Building? *In:* G. Bankoff, T. Cannon, F. Kruger, B. Orlowski, and E.L.F. Schipper, eds. *Cultures and Disasters: Understanding Cultural Framings in Disaster Risk Reduction*. Abingdon: Routledge.

Schroeder, Kristy Bergman. 2016. "Religion and Secularism in Development:" Trends in the Approaches of Bilateral Donors in Canada and the United Kingdom. Master of Arts, Winnipeg: The University of Manitoba. https://mspace.lib. umanitoba.ca/xmlui/handle/1993/32029.

Stirk, C., 2015. *An Act of Faith: Humanitarian Financing and Zakat*. Bristol: Global Humanitarian Assistance (GHA), Briefing Paper.

Stoddard, A., 2003. *Humanitarian NGOs: Challenges and Trends*. London: ODI Humanitarian Policy Group, No. HPG Briefing Number 12.

Taylor, C., 2007. *A Secular Age*. Harvard: Harvard University Press.

Taylor, Charles. 2008. "Buffered and Porous Selves." *The Immanent Frame* (blog). September 2, 2008. https://tif.ssrc.org/2008/09/02/buffered-and-porous-selves/.

Taylor, Glynn, Abby Stoddard, Adele Harmer, Katherine Harver, and Paul Harvey. 2012. "The State of the Humanitarian System, 2012 Edition." London: ALNAP, Overseas Development Institute (ODI).

Tomalin, E., 2013. *Religions and Development*. London: Routledge.

Tomalin, E., 2015. Gender, Development, and the "De-privatisation" of Religion: Reframing Feminism and Religion in Asia. *In: Religion and the Politics of Development*. London: Palgrave Macmillan, 61–82.

Walsh, T. 2012. Religion, Peace and the Post-Secular Public Sphere. *International Journal on World Peace, Vol. XXIX, No. 2*, 35–61.

Watanabe, C., 2015. The Politics of Nonreligious Aid: A Japanese Environmental Ethic in Myanmar. *In: Religion and the Politics of Development*. London: Palgrave Macmillan, 225–242.

Wilkinson, Olivia. 2014. "Is There a Secular Humanitarian Faith?" *The Religion Factor* (blog). September 24, 2014. https://www.rug.nl/research/centre-for-religious-studies/religion-conflict-globalization/blog/is-there-a-secular-humanitarian-faith-24-09-2014.

Wilson, E.K., 2012. *After Secularism: Rethinking Religion in Global Politics*. Basingstoke: Palgrave Macmillan.

3 How people affected by disaster understand religious dynamics in the humanitarian system

When I spoke to people following Typhoon Haiyan, they expressed that religious belief and practice had been a central part of their disaster experience, but external organisations had not always heeded their requests related to time for prayer, reconstruction of religious buildings, and other aspects of this folding of religion into the overall experience of the disaster and response to it. While the voices of disaster-affected people are too frequently unheard as part of humanitarian response, examining people's opinions of secular humanitarian organisations helps to reveal the many misconceptions of humanitarian "beneficiaries." Likewise, while disaster risk reduction professionals are increasingly encouraged to take cultural nuance into account (Cannon *et al.* 2014; Bankoff *et al.* 2015; Browne and Olson 2019), the vast expanse of what can be termed "religious" can make it intimidating for aid organisations to respond. Leading from a desire to foreground the experiences of people affected by disaster, this chapter explores disaster and post-disaster experiences recounted in focus groups conducted in 2015.

To help conceptualise religion in disaster, this chapter uses Woodhead's "Five Concepts of Religion" (Woodhead 2011) as a framework for understanding religious beliefs and practices in relations to disasters and humanitarian response. I challenge the idea that religious belief leads to a mainly fatalistic perception of risk and disaster (Bankoff 2004; Schipper 2015), as people unravel their theologically nuanced and socially conditioned positions that prompted them to action, rather than causing them to be passive. Cultural dissonance was also a common experience for disaster-affected people receiving assistance from external organisations following Haiyan, as has been highlighted by several studies following the disaster (Corpus *et al.* 2015; Field 2016, 2017). Cultural dissonance around values and power differentials has been found to be common across many disaster contexts (Browne 2015; Lin and Lin 2016): the cultural aspects of dissonance may be different in each case but the experience of dissonance and misunderstanding remains the same as external actors proceed without due attention to the attitudes and practices of those they are aiming to help, potentially causing more harm to these people as they struggle with recovering from the disaster and managing the demands of external assistance.

Religions and disasters in the Philippines

Scholars argue that the Philippines has a type of culture of disaster (Bankoff 2003) or disaster sub-culture (Luna 2003). For Bankoff, this is the widely recognised undercurrent of Filipino culture that is "shaped by the threat of hazard" (Bankoff 2003, p. 162). A recurrent theme in discussion of Filipino characteristics in the face of disaster is resilience. Jose Rizal, a national hero for his struggles against Spanish colonialism, stated that the Filipino character is like bamboo in that it bends but will bounce back (Robles 1991, pp. 1, 6 in Bankoff 2003, p. 170). Many have debated the range of qualities that are particularly present in the Philippines, but there are four aspects of the Filipino character that are commonly stated, summarised by Ignacio and Perlas (1994, p. 55), as *bayanihan*/community cooperation/*pakikipagkapwa,* strong family/social networks, religion/spirituality/prayers, and humour/laughter.

Much of what is expressed in the first two points is highly interrelated. Strong networks for social cooperation that exist between Filipinos to help in times of hardship include unions, clubs, and People's Organisations, among others. Overseas workers provide much support in remittances. A sense of communality, or "*pagkikipagkapwa,*" is central to the mobilisation of support from others in the community following disaster (Gaillard, Liamzon, and Maceda 2005, p. 57) as "people's sense of self is most intensely relational" (Corpus *et al.* 2015, p. 8). Mangarin (2013, p. 48) goes as far to say that, "Filipinos generally do not value individualism as much as they do social relations." Luna (2003, p. 3) explains *bayanihan* as "voluntarily providing help and support to a person in need in the community." *Utang na loob*, or debt of gratitude, is central to this as a moral principle that binds people together after help has been given. These are more than expressions of unity and togetherness, but distinct statements that one will "[toil] on another's behalf and [assume] another's burdens" (Bankoff 2007, p. 28). These systems of mutual assistance are under threat from the influence of modernisation, including economic fragmentation and migration (Hilhorst *et al.* 2015, pp. 514–515). As a recent representative survey of adults in the Philippines found, 79% revealed they were concerned by disasters. Notably, while 74% stated they were active in a civil society association, 68% said they "rarely work with others to improve community life," 69% said they "never or rarely participate in local activities or events," and only 2.5–4% said they had received support from various community structures, such as neighbours, friends, and the broader community following a disaster (Bollettino *et al.* 2018, p. 21), suggesting further isolation and fragmentation of previously strong community coping structures that make up the Philippines' culture of disaster.

The third point about religion, spirituality, and prayer contains complex notions that touch upon many theological and sociological concepts. The idea of pain and sacrifice is particularly noteworthy in relation to the mix of Catholicism and traditional religion in the Philippines, particularly as it relates to the experience of disaster. Hilhorst et al. see the use of traditional ritual and religion as a coping mechanism in disaster (Hilhorst et al. 2015, p. 515). Mercado (2000, p. viii) explains that in Filipino myths "one cannot go to a higher form of life without giving up something of the present life. And the giving up entails pain." Following on, Hornedo (in Mercado 2000, p. 109) asserts that *pagpapakasakit*, the notion of sacrifice, is "embedded deep in the traditional culture" of the Philippines in the idea that you must lose something to rise to a higher level. In the Filipino context, we think of the sacrifices made by those that have experienced disaster. Mangarin (2013, p. 23) frames her explanation of the Catholic Church of the Philippines in this light, reminding us that the Church of today "emerged from these stories of people struggling to find the meaning of their faith especially in moments of difficulties and hardships." The Church does not only come to aid those in need but has itself been formed by disaster and the sacrifices made during those times. The Church is part of the culture of disaster. A clear example is shown in the history of the Manila Cathedral. It has been rebuilt eight times following earthquakes, typhoons, fire, and conflict (de la Cruz 2015). In his speech to Pope Francis during his visit to the Philippines in January 2015, the Archbishop of Manila, Cardinal Tagle, used the history of the Cathedral to explain Filipino resilience. He said,

> This cathedral has been razed to the ground many times, but it refuses to vanish. It boldly rises from the ruins – just like the Filipino people. Yes, Holy Father, we bishops, priests and religious men and women have seen and lived the suffering and determination of our people. "We are afflicted in every way possible, but we are not crushed" (2 Corinthians 4:8).
>
> (Cardinal Tagle 2015)

Cardinal Tagle goes on to say, in the same speech, that faith is one of the main foundations of Filipino resilience, bolstered by the Pope's visit after Haiyan. The use of prayer is specifically highlighted as one of the most fundamental aspects of the Philippine religious experience for coping with disaster. Bankoff (2007, p. 28) gives the example of the people around Mount

Pinatubo who, following its eruption, used Christian prayer and shamanistic ritual to protect themselves from the flows of lahar that swept down from the side of the volcano at regular intervals and spread destruction in their villages. Both Carandang (1996) and Wong-Fernandez (1996) accompanied survivors of disasters in the Philippines and documented the ways in which prayer was central to their recovery. In research with 2,020 older adults (over 65) following Typhoon Haiyan, (Almazan *et al.* 2018) found that spirituality and a positive attitude were the two strongest factors associated with disaster resilience in this age group, which was also a group that displayed a high level of disaster resilience in general.

The fourth coping mechanism recognised in Filipino culture is humour and laughter. Luna (2003, p. 24) sees this coping mechanism as part of the disaster subculture that has trained people to act jovially in the face of calamity. Studies in other contexts have shown that both spirituality and humour are associated with positive coping mechanisms following disaster (Cherry *et al.* 2018). There is some debate that another concept, "*bahala na*" (literally, "leave it to fate") is also a key coping mechanism, or, in fact, preparedness measure, in the face of disaster in the Philippines. Bankoff (2003, p. 167, 2007, p. 28), Gaillard, Liamzon, and Maceda (2005, p. 53), and Ignacio and Perlas (1994, p. 51) all view this idea as more than just fatalism. Instead, it includes the more complex idea of taking calculated risks, rather than taking a simple fatalistic approach. One of the more active aspects of *bahala na*, Bankoff reminds us, is the use of prayer. As he puts it (2003, p. 167), *bahala na* involves belief in the "efficacy of prayer and in the intercession of divine protection." This moves the debate from the sociological to the more theological: if all events are within God's will and plan for the world, "good fortune and tragedy are thus coloured with some degree of optimism" (Ignacio and Perlas 1994, p. 51). Ignacio thinks, therefore, that *bahala na* is not "a defeatist resignation," but "a reservoir of psychic energy, a psychological prop which Filipino's lean on in time of difficulty." Although *bahala na* might encourage people to take risks, it also helps them "accept tragedy because disaster can occur despite their best efforts of human and divine intervention" (Bankoff 2007, p. 28). Bankoff argues that although people's behaviours may appear strange and overly risky, they have contextually based decision-making frameworks that are appropriate to their situation in such an environment (Bankoff 2003, p. 162). We are reminded that although an act, such as prayer, may only be viewed as a basic, or even pointless, method of coping through the eyes of secular humanitarian aid workers, it is a widely used and highly influential bedrock of recovery for many Filipinos.

While criticised by Rizal as part of colonial oppression in the 1800s (Alatas in Alatas and Sinha 2017, pp. 147, 163–164), the Roman Catholic Church in the Philippines has more recently committed to acting as a "church of the poor," in line with the move towards a preferential option for the poor underlined in Vatican II, and spurred on, at least in part, by the activity of priests, nuns, and lay people for the protection and freedom of the poor during the Marcos regime (Holden 2015). Religious institutions have long been involved in disaster relief efforts in the Philippines. The Church is recognised among the range of organisations that help following disasters (Luna 2006, p. 3). Not only do churches act as a central focal point of community activity following trauma (Crittenden and Rodolfo 2002, p. 57), the Roman Catholic Church has many organisations that are highly involved in civil society in the Philippines. As Moreno (2006, p. 10) points out, its organisations "are civil society actors in as much as they are relatively autonomous and organised operating within the public sphere, the space between the state and households. This overlap blurs the distinction between the church and civil society." At the national level, the Catholic Bishops Conference of the Philippines (CBCP) has its National Secretariat for Social Action (NASSA) or Caritas Philippines (part of the larger Caritas Internationalist network). The local branches that focus on service are called Diocesan Social Action Centres (DSACs) and have been crucial actors in much of the response and rehabilitation work conducted following Haiyan. Even more locally, Basic Ecclesial Communities (BECs) are formed by congregation members as groups in which they can worship, teach, and serve other community members (Mangarin, DC 2013, p. 28; Bankoff 2015, p. 434). They often have a special focus on the poor and marginalised as they are formed as part of "a participatory church with preferential option for the poor" (Abinales 2003, pp. 156–157). DSACs, BECs, and other affiliated groupings install early warning systems (Garcia 2010), provide education and information on sustainable development, climate change adaptation, disaster risk reduction, and other such topics following the Church's social justice teaching (Magalang 2010), and deliver other activities that NGOs usually provide. However, there are also other activities they are involved such as bible-sharing (often on themes of Disaster Risk Reduction (DRR) and other development and humanitarian related themes) (Magalang 2010, pp. 81, 85), rituals (such as organising blessings of reconstructed houses) (Gaspar 2014), and spending time listening to the stories of affected populations (Mangarin 2013, p. 113; Gaspar 2014). Local Disaster Response Committees and community organisations can also evolve from BECs (Bankoff 2015, pp. 434, 438). The fact that these organisations are supported by the Church and part of its services is also reported to make these activities highly credible to the local population (Magalang 2010, p. 89).

Evangelical churches are growing in the Philippines. Aldrovandi describes difficulties in defining the term evangelical, likening Evangelicalism not to

a single vessel majestically transporting a unified community of believers to political domination, social redemption, and eternal salvation . . .
[but] a vast fleet of rowboats and boogie boards, each bearing an individual in search of an authentic personal experience with God.

(Aldrovandi 2014, p. 131)

The highly decentralised and personalised nature of belief in evangelical
churches stands in contrast to the dominance of the Catholic Church with its
hierarchical structures in the Philippines. As with some countries in Africa
and other Southeast Asian countries, the Pentecostal movement has been in
"conflict and competition" with the Catholic Church (Moreno 2006, p. 16).
As regards disaster, many of the more fundamentalist churches have an
eschatological reading of earthquakes, typhoons, volcanic eruptions, and
other events, seeing them as a sign of the "end times." Woods (2002, p. 24),
in research on the Philippines in particular, points out that this changes the
way in which they view social action. He notes, "Baptists view the church
as a first aid station rather than a hospital, i.e. there is little time to heal social
problems. Their goal is to get as many as they can to respond to a public
invitation and say a prayer [to convert]." While this is not always the case,
evangelical churches, usually smaller and with less funding, are less vis-
ible in disasters and development in the country. Haiyan increased the work
of international Protestant-based agencies and also brought in new actors.
These organisations invigorated some of the social work of the Protestant
churches in the country. Acknowledging that there is a substantial Muslim
community in the Philippines with accompanying Civil Society Organisations (CSOs) (Buckley 2017, p. 163) involved in humanitarian and development work, the Visayan region, where the Typhoon hit, has a very small
Muslim population and there were no Muslim focus group participants.
Particularly on some of the islands there are also Indigenous religions and
varying levels of syncretism was communicated by research participants.

But what of the secular within this mix? Although it is reported that church
attendance figures are declining, particularly among young people and after
the "holier-than-thou" postulating that surrounded the Reproductive Health
Bill debates in the Philippines in 2013 (Cornelio and Sapitula 2015), it is
far from being a largely secularised nation. For one, Cornelio and Sapitula
(2015) report that religiosity is not declining and that lower Catholic Church
attendance figures only show the success of Evangelistic zeal in converting
Catholics to Protestantism. Likewise, church attendance is not necessarily
indicative of religiosity, with over 93.5% of the population saying they have
always believed in God (Smith 2012, p. 7, in Cornelio and Sapitula 2015)
and the "sustained religiosity of Philippine society" (Cornelio 2014, p. 488).
Sapitula sees a growing secular voice in the Philippines, particularly since

the debate on the Reproductive Health Bill, but also underlines the complexity of Filipino religiosity, with dual belonging ("wherein individuals do not perceive their religious membership in exclusive terms") common and advocates for "deep pluralism" that moves away from monolithic thinking (Sapitula 2015, pp. 4–5). When secularity does appear, it is often at odds with the culture and must adapt. Clarke and Jennings (2008, p. 3) tell of a secular NGO in the Philippines that starts its meetings with prayers. They say, "Any NGO or development agency that seeks work in and with this community [in the Philippines] must engage with its faith identity and the [faith-based] community organisations to which it gives rise."

Typhoon Haiyan

The impact of Haiyan not only left a physical mark on the Visayan region, but a trail of trauma and emotional stress. It was reported that, in the absence of enough morgues, people would bring their dead to churches (Workman 2013). Religiosity was found in memorial services for the dead led by local leaders (although they were not necessarily religious ceremonies) (Quirino 2014). It has been reported that many of the affected people have become more religious after the typhoon and church attendance has gone up (Esteban 2015, p. 19; Hearth 2015). Those within the Church have advocated that the recovery from Haiyan can demonstrate the extent to which the Church is united (Sadowski 2014). Others say that people have always been resilient, and this is thanks to their faith (Martin 2013).

FBOs were highly involved from the beginning of the response and often "filled the gaps in relief" (Darcy *et al.* 2015, p. 24). Religious congregations were present when other facilities could not be found. For example, a chapel was used as an examination room by midwives in Tacloban as it was the only structure that survived the typhoon in the locality (Barmania 2014, p. 1198). There were some limited reports of the ways in which secular organisations adapted. For example, the International Organisation for Migration (IOM) posted a blog about a priest blessing a new X-Ray machine they had provided for a hospital (IOM 2015). Mostly, however, the reports detailed the ways in which secular organisations had failed to understand local cultural nuances. Reproductive health, a contested area in which boundaries around contraception, the morning after pill, and other such medicine is still hotly debated, especially by the Church, was "not easy to sell to humanitarian agencies" who shied away from this area (Barmania 2014, p. 1198).

Feedback from communities also demonstrated that they perceived INGOs and NNGOs very differently. As Featherstone (2014, p. 16) reports on one of the discussions conducted for his research,

In Leyte, the Barangay Chairperson used the Visayan term *"mitabang"* (to help) to describe the assistance of the INGOs but used the term *"miuban namo"* (to journey with us) to describe the assistance provided by NNGOs, and similar terminology was used by community leaders in other parts of affected areas. For them, engagement is about building a relationship rather than the simple provision of assistance.

There was a qualitative difference among organisations demonstrated in the way they provided assistance, not the quantities provided.

Finally, the visit of Pope Francis in January 2015 was a powerful reminder of the place of religion in disaster and response. Hundreds of thousands of people flocked to his open-air mass at Tacloban airport, the very site of one of the most devastating storm surges during Haiyan, while another tropical storm approached the city (Thomson Reuters 2015). He spoke briefly yet powerfully saying,

> So many of you have lost everything. I don't know what to say to you. But the Lord does know what to say to you. Some of you have lost part of your families. All I can do is keep silence and walk with you all with my silent heart. Many of you have asked the Lord – why lord? And to each of you, to your heart, Christ responds with his heart from the cross. I have no more words for you. Let us look to Christ. He is the Lord. He understands us because he underwent all the trials that we, that you, have experienced.
>
> (Pope Francis 2015a)

Pope Francis was forced to leave early as the new storm approached, but the people were not discouraged as they faced up to yet another natural hazard threatening their city. The storm was not as strong as feared, Pope Francis safely flew out of Tacloban, and the people of the city continued their lives, buoyed up by their most recent visitor.

Religious experience after Typhoon Haiyan as aspects of culture, practice, relationship, and identity

Rather than reaching for an exacting definition of religion, Linda Woodhead proposes five concepts for religion (Woodhead 2011) that denote the most commonly employed uses of the term: religion as culture, identity, relationship, practice, and power. Each of Woodhead's five main concepts unravels into smaller specifics. She believes that this is a better approach than an exact definition as it allows for complexity and interrelated elements to become clear. Following Woodhead's lead, I analysed these aspects of religion for their relationship to disaster in general, selecting those of most relevance from Woodhead's longer list, and linked them to classical theories about religion and in relation to findings from speaking with disaster-affected people following Typhoon Haiyan.

Religion as culture: meaning and cultural order

From Woodhead's category we take the idea of religion as explaining the incomprehensible. Frazer and Freud famously focused on the idea of religion as comfort when faced with the incomprehensible. Frazer's (2009) work argues that religion exists because it helps to explain otherwise incomprehensible events by relying on the unseen. This is important to remember in terms of the post-disaster situation where events could often be described as incomprehensible due to huge devastation and loss of life. The 'seen' is so devastating that a turn to the 'unseen' is needed to comprehend events. Freud (2008) furthered this idea by detailing his belief that religion is an illusion, a response to the forces of nature and the weaknesses of humans. Although both widely criticised, Frazer and Freud, usefully for our purposes in the disaster context, begin to highlight the idea that religion can come to the fore in response to the fear of chaos and meaninglessness.

Durkheim advanced the idea that religion is a social institution that has been created by society to support itself, especially in times of need. Durkheim's focal concepts are often reduced into two simple statements: society is the soul of religion and society is the "Godhead." These two phrases express Durkheim's belief that society creates religion *sui generis* (from itself) so that the "totem" or "Godhead" the society comes to consider as sacred and worthy of veneration is actually itself. For Durkheim, it is collectiveness that is of real importance to religion, hence his postulation that "society is the soul of religion" (Durkheim 1915). Peter Berger takes up Durkheim's idea of society creating religion. He explains that everyday life is put under the "sacred canopy" of meaning. This harks back to the idea that humans are most profoundly afraid of chaos and meaninglessness. To ensure that this abyss of meaninglessness is kept as far away as possible the society goes through a process of "world-construction." Berger (1967, p. 22) argues that, "Men are congenitally compelled to impose a meaningful order upon reality. . . . Every nomos [religion, in this context] is an edifice created in the face of the potent and alien force of chaos. This chaos must be kept at bay at all costs." The entire social institution of religion provides that reassurance for its members at any point and therefore individuals abide by this social institution so that they are shielded from the possibility of meaninglessness and chaos.

Empirical research from Falk in Thailand following the 2004 Indian Ocean tsunami recounts the crucial position of Buddhist monks in providing interpretation of the disaster to survivors by giving meaning to the event as well as the psychological encouragement provided by these members of the religious community to help people emotionally recover (Falk 2014, pp. 125–127). In Pakistan, Cheema *et al.* (2014, pp. 2219–2220) describe the role of Imams after an earthquake as "faith healers who lead the way to spiritual healing for their affected communities" by providing both individual and community counselling. These examples show the real-world applicability of religion as supplying meaning and cultural order following disaster.

From speaking with typhoon-affected people in the Philippines, it was clear that meaning making through the lens of faith was one way in which people in the affected area interpreted the disaster following the typhoon. People gave meaning to the disaster through their faith from a range of angles. They saw the typhoon as part of God's plan, meaning that it was not a random act of destruction but had a place as part of a greater plan. Some people thought that the typhoon was a sign from God for people to turn back to religion. Others thought that their survival was a sure sign of God's grace. Others thanked God for the disaster because it helped strengthen their faith or it was a test of their faith. From Frazer, this relates to the notion that the disaster event (the seen event) was so incomprehensible that recourse to the unseen (the divine) is needed for comprehension and peace of mind.

One man, who attended an evangelical church, gave a vivid description of his own dismay with God and then return following the typhoon. He said,

[After the typhoon] So many Christians ask the Lord why . . . [I] pray to the Lord "why why why?" So the Lord spoke to me. . . . His promise says to me that He has a plan. So I pray to the Lord, Lord forgive me. Then I realise that it's our purpose so I give it up to the Lord and I say Lord I will obey you whatever you bring. So I notice that the Lord loves me so much. . . . And I said to the Lord thank you so much. From this very day I will bring this good news to the people. You are so very good, you are a loving God. From that time until now I know He will not leave our family. He is very good. Even with our needs He will provide.

The man described how he found solace in, as he believed, a direct explanation from God that the event had meaning as part of God's plan and he should not give up hope because God loves him. Other research conducted following Haiyan also found that religious struggles were a part of people's disaster recovery experience. In one study with 1,929 respondents from Bantayan Island it was found that, although apostasy and anger at

God was low across the participants, a significant minority had struggled with their emotions towards God, and this was influenced by related factors including "education level, socio-economic status, denomination, barangay, loss of loved ones in the disaster, format of post-disaster church fellowship meetings, and the importance of God in their lives prior to the disaster" (O'Connell *et al.* 2017, p. 330). Across the people I spoke to, there was only one instance in which an older woman stated that she struggled to use religion as a source for meaning making. She had been in one of the most profoundly affected areas, losing her daughter and daughter's family, including grandchildren. She said her heart was empty. We cannot take a homogeneous approach that sees religion as a constant source of meaning making in disaster, but only recognise its widespread influence.

A notable aspect of people's interpretations was that INGOs played a role in this meaning making. The humanitarian system, as secular as it may be, was imbued with a spiritual significance in that it was seen to be part of God's plan and the arrival of INGOs was another reason to give thanks to God. One man said, "The NGOs were sent by God to do what the government has not. It should be the government's responsibility to help prepare for the disaster – they have made promises, but they have done nothing." The government gaps were filled by God, through the work of INGOs. This sense of gratitude, linked to the concept of *utang na loob*, was a key sub-theme in this meaning making. Even if something bad had happened to them, the interpretation was to give thanks to God that there had not been something worse visited upon their family.

Yet INGOs did not necessarily understand how to connect to this meaning making, which resulted in inappropriate assistance. The most notable case, in this regard, was that of psychosocial assistance that had been given in one community. They had been severely affected and had had psychosocial sessions with various different organisations. One woman recounted how she had preferred the session given by a local team of psychologists who had formed to help people after Yolanda. She said it was focused on the psychological and spiritual. She said that, otherwise, she had taken her son to sessions from various organisations, including the government, where the same secular module with the same exercises was used each time and they repeated what had been done before without much success. In another focus group, a few other people mentioned that the psychosocial assistance they had received had just been a few games with the children, but that they felt a spiritual side was missing from this. In another community, there was a conversation about whether they would consider talking within an organisation to let them know about other needs around the psychosocial and spiritual. They confessed that they would be hesitant to bring this up, noting that they talk about it among themselves, but they would not volunteer this information unless specifically asked. This demonstrates one the reasons why it can be difficult for organisations to uncover the psychosocial needs in a community.

As this was seen to be part of God's plan, a belief in divine intervention helped underline the meaning making people found from their faith about the disaster. There were some divides between Catholic and evangelical interpretations, however. On the one hand interpreted as a direct act of God to give a sign about the last days and "end of times" by evangelical research participants, on the other hand the typhoon was not attributed to God in this direct way by Catholic respondents but instead the focus was on smaller events that were seen as miracles in answer to prayer, for example, being in just the right spot so that a family was not killed by a tree that fell on the building in which they were sheltering from the typhoon.

Schipper outlines nine entry points for examining religion in the context of disaster risk reduction and adaptation to climate change (Schipper 2015, p. 152) for improved resilience. The first set of three focus on capacity:

A-1 Role of religion in supporting development;
A-2 Role of religion in encouraging social capital (organisation) for coping during difficult times;
A-3 Role of religion in influencing preventive and reactive responses to disaster risk and climate change.

The second set of three focus on reducing risk:

B-1 Role of religion in influencing policy on environment and climate change (positively);
B-2 Role of religion in raising vulnerability to hazards;
B-3 Role of religion in reducing vulnerability to hazards.

The final set focuses on responding to disasters:

C-1 Role of religion in helping people to emotionally overcome disaster (mental health);
C-2 Role of religious institutions in supporting disaster relief and recovery processes;
C-3 Role of religion in influencing relief and recovery processes (rebuilding, planning).

While acknowledging that religion can increase vulnerability to hazards, Schipper also outlines the ways in which it can provide strength and add to people's disaster resilience, both in risk reduction and preparedness as well as post-disaster strength. Schipper's categorisation C-1 was particularly of note in research results. The mental strength people found in their faith was a common concept. This psychological strength was about staying calm, diminishing their fear, and not falling apart in front of others (staying strong for their family and friends). Likewise, religious belief and practice were about being a good person, being honest, respectful, and persevering. Women particularly highlighted this aspect of their faith in building their strength. For men, it was noted that they felt a lot of pressure after the typhoon, with one man saying that he would have gone "insane" without his faith. Instead, his faith helped him stay sane and face up to the long-recovery period ahead of him.

B-2 and B-3 are of note because of their interrelated nature. While the fatalistic impulses of religious believers have been commented on by others as dangerous for their disaster risk perception (in the Philippines, Bankoff 2004) and therefore part of category B-2, the majority of participants qualified fatalistic statements with stories of preparedness, learning for the future, and resilience. In this way, this research did not find anyone who had a purely fatalistic, leave-it-all-to-God attitude. Even if they thought that suffering is part of life or that these were disasters sent by God then they would still think that it was necessary to be prepared. Even for those of an evangelical faith, who one might expect to be the most fatalistic with their interpretation, saw that their need to be prepared and learn for the future was part of God's will to give them "presence of mind" during disaster.

This notably challenges traditional definitions of different interpretations of disasters as acts of God, nature, or man. While the definitions of disasters as acts of nature and man have been worked on intensively over the years to build frameworks of understanding for disasters that include the complex interweaving of hazards and vulnerabilities, many classifications will still simply equate the Act of God perspective with that of a fatalistic attitude. A person can hold many seeming contradictions within themselves: both fatalistic in that they think God has a plan for them and when their time will come *and* motivated to reduce their vulnerabilities for future disaster events; both viewing the typhoon as part of God's plan *and* an effect of human generated climate change.

Religion, spirituality, and prayer were ever present in this mix, but as one part of the whole rather than separate. Having said this, faith was also represented by participants as foremost in this construction of the whole. People said that their faith was "first," "the most important" or "the very best foundation" in life. This was not mutually exclusive with people's prioritisation of material needs as well, such as shelter and livelihood. In fact, faith acted as an umbrella notion, motivating and protecting while they attended to a multitude of needs (Wilkinson 2015, p. 25). In response to some authors' descriptions of Filipinos as settling for less by relying on ideas of good or bad luck, coping rather than solutions, and complacency rather than activity (Sison 2014), there was some indication that people felt they must be patient, count blessings, and be thankful for what they had rather than demanding more.

Religion as culture: tradition and memory

From Woodhead's category we take the idea of religion as having a survival value through tradition and memory. Malinowski and Hervieu-Leger emphasise the use of religion to survive catastrophe. Malinowski discusses religion and groups in times of crisis. Malinowski recognised that death can have a profound disintegrating result on a society if its effects are not dealt with and he postulates that religion aids humans in two ways. First, Malinowski talks of the "survival value" of religious tradition, stating that "The primitive man's share of knowledge, his social fabric, his customs and beliefs, are the invaluable yield of devious experience of his forefathers, bought at an extravagant price and to be maintained at any cost" (Malinowski 1974, p. 29). Although Malinowski's focus on "primitive man" is now extremely dated, his postulation emphasises the experiences of pain and suffering of previous generations bound in tradition. Tradition in this sense is the inbuilt coping strategy present within society. To bring us to slightly more contemporary debate, Hervieu-Léger (2000) postulated, that religion is a string of collective memory. This chain of memory bridges the gap between the individual and the community and the present and the past. Institutionalised collective memory brings individuals together to form one cohesive group that is self-perpetuating as the memory chain carries on to the next generation and continues the social institution of religion. It is therefore of upmost importance for the society to maintain these traditions so that the wisdom held within is not lost.

There is a trend in the study of disaster risk reduction, which examines how indigenous knowledge can be integrated with scientific knowledge to improve prevention, preparedness, and mitigation of the impact of natural hazards, particularly in small islands developing states where earthquakes, tsunamis, and typhoons can be particularly calamitous (Mercer *et al.* 2009; Lauer 2012). People also find much security in the continuation of the normal functioning of religious communities. For example, Cheema et al. found that some communities, after the 2005 earthquake in Pakistan, preferred their Imams to only perform their religious duties rather than other relief and rehabilitation tasks (Cheema *et al.* 2014, p. 2216). It is the authority of religious leaders that can be particularly influential in organising affected populations after disaster. For example, the uptake of activities such as quarantine in Ebola (Featherstone 2015, p. 39) or chlorination of water to fight water-borne diseases (Aten *et al.* 2015, p. 20) has been reported to be more effective when done through the authority of local faith communities. Following Haiyan, people felt the importance of religious tradition and a consequent responsibility to uphold and maintain tradition. This related to tensions in Filipino society around secularisation and shifts in religious affiliation. People from the affected population described their anxiety about the loss of knowledge about religious practices, such as saying the rosary, among young people. While the typhoon was seen as an event that drew people back to the church and so bolstered the place of religion in society, some also confessed that this could not hide the fact that there had been an overall drop in congregation numbers at Catholic churches. Both Catholic and evangelical congregations claimed that their numbers had swelled in the immediate aftermath of the typhoon, although Catholic people saw this as a turn towards tradition and memory for feelings of comfort and the survival value of religion, whereas evangelical respondents did not, of course, have the same ties to tradition and were forward looking in aims to plant more churches and save more people within an eschatological framework.

Linked to this is the need for organisations to understand the local culture and beliefs so that they can be in touch with what needs are present. As noted by NGO staff, people were hesitant to criticise at first and would often say that their needs had been met and they were thankful to God for providing for their needs. After further conversation, other responses emerged. Several groups said that provision from local FBOs had been the first to arrive because they were already in situ or nearby. A few others said that these groups, through their church, were the people they asked for assistance from, in a way that large INGOs are not immediately accessible to affected populations. People said that they had not been asked about the cultural and spiritual aspects of their lives by organisations. However, they did say that such questions would be appreciated. One community said that the organisation that had helped the most in the area, which happened to be an FBO in this instance, really knew the concerns of the community because they asked more questions with consultations. They said that knowing the real concerns and issues in the community meant that the organisations knew how to really build resilience and also make programmes sustainable. This was echoed in another community, which had happened to be helped by a secular organisation. In this case they explained how they had worked with the organisation to best accommodate their shelter needs while still remaining as close to the shoreline as possible for their livelihood. In both cases, it was not the secularity or faith base creating the positive perception of the organisation, but the amount of interaction the organisations had with the communities. This has been called "adopted" communities in other Hai-yan research, in which both faith-based and secular organisations were also involved (Corpus *et al*. 2015, p. 36).

Religion as relationship and identity: social relations, community creation, and stewardship

The religious community provides the individual with a coping strategy after disaster. Religion provides a community of people with whom one can discuss ordeals, reconnect with the religious ideas of life after death, and be lifted out of their individual concerns in the collective experience. Religion acts as one of the cultural systems through which social relations in post-disaster scenarios can occur. Within the relationship between believers a strong sense of personal identity and community develops. This is not religion at the societal level, such as in relation to politics, but at "micro-level interactions" (Woodhead 2011, p. 133). This is also intricately linked to Woodhead's category of religion as power, most particularly the subdivision of religious resources. As she notes, following Durkheim, "Ritual gatherings may serve to co-ordinate individual actions, generate power-fully motivating and solidaristic emotions, overcome fear and doubt, and regularly renew bonds and sentiments" (Woodhead 2011, p. 135). This is theologically reflected in the notion of stewardship, which is found across religious traditions, and encourages people "to move away from straight-forward self-interest . . . to become 'social stewards' who look beyond themselves towards improving conditions for the wider community" (Fiddian-Qasmiyeh and Ager 2013, p. 5). Likewise, religion can provide trained leaders, volunteers, and infrastructure that can support communities (Fiddian-Qasmiyeh and Ager 2013). These are all powerful resources that religion may have to offer that other institutions cannot post-disaster.

The notion of loving your neighbour was a basis for community strength, as was the importance of familial love, for people following Haiyan. As precepts of religious belief, love for each other was a demonstration of God's love, through the eyes of respondents. Familial love was most commonly mentioned by women, community support was more equally divided among genders, while men more frequently mentioned their faith in relation to supporting their working practices and personal mental health. The interlinking concepts of love, sacrifice, and trust are core elements adding to the idea of faith as central for personal and community strength. Their love was demonstrated in their willingness to make sacrifices. Only Catholic respondents brought up the word "sacrifice." It had both positive and negative connotations. In some ways, it was a resource spurred by faith that allowed people to cope with the damages and disappointments they had suffered. Yet in other ways this was always tinged with notes of dependence and obligation. In order to be a faithful person, you must sacrifice, but sometimes that sacrifice included actions that disempowered them. One example from a community in Tacloban, which had seen the largest influx of INGOs, was their sacrifice of time and effort needed in order to benefit from NGOs (who require participation, forms, lines, and an increasing level of bureaucracy with no guarantee of receiving aid at the end of initial assessments). When people felt they had no power, they turned it into a positive, i.e., that they were willing to make sacrifices.

Stewardship was another notable way in which faith was part of community relations in the post-disaster context. The theological notion of stewardship is based on the idea that God created the earth, therefore has ownership of it, and as part of God's creation, humans must act as stewards of it and faithful servants to God. In practice, this can relate to the act of tithing, giving to and helping others but also, in particular reference to the natural world, a form of environmentalism. The position of the Philippines as one of the countries at the forefront of effects of climate change here meets with the dominant religious cultural context of the country. Catholic respondents very much saw climate change as man-made, as a failure of humans to act as good stewards and fulfil our responsibilities to safeguarding the earth in this regard. One man explained how the environment around him had changed over time, with the heat of the sun increasing and the loss of trees after the typhoon. He unequivocally stated that climate change was man's fault. Another man summed this up, saying,

> If we try to ask [why] God do this to us? But we never think also that we the people are caretakers of this environment and this world. We are the stewards of God's blessings and God's nature. But sometimes we never try to think about how beautiful this world is. So we threw things without thinking what will happen to the future generations. The garbage in the sea, in the open canal, and it comes back to us. We don't question God, we question why we do this. We have to follow and take good care of this world, by doing things properly. Not burning the plastic to make fumes. The ozone layer is thinning now because of the toxic fumes going up.

This shows how religious principles, personal faith, and views on climate change coexist in people's minds. As some of the people in the world who have experienced first-hand the devastating effects of climate change, they are well versed in the problems facing the planet. Within this understanding, their religious beliefs were one of the central explanatory tools. The idea of stewardship, of being stewards of the world that God created for humans, was part of this. One woman explained this as such,

> As of now, only last Tuesday, Father gave the penitential service in our barangay, he said that Pope Benedict was writing seven dangerous sins, one of this is about our world. The people must know what is happening today about global warming, about the climate change. If you know this, we have already, we are educated, I think the people will be strong enough to face all the calamities we experience.

When she spoke, the rest of the focus group gave a spontaneous round of applause. She underlines that knowledge and education are vital in building people's awareness and capacities. Notably, it is through church services that she has gained this knowledge, thus intermingling religious belief with scientific explanations. These focus groups took place before Laudato Si, Pope Francis' encyclical on climate change (Pope Francis 2015b), which prompted further education in this area from the pulpit. People thought that their faith worked through them to make them more active in the face of climate change. One man said his faith made him work faster, "it moves in thoughts and words and in the heart. If we have faith, things will go smoothly and we can move freely." Others said that their faith helped them not to worry even though they knew that there would still be "drastic effects of climate change." One woman joked that her hair had gone grey from climate change.

In contrast, evangelical groups did not permit that climate change was man made. One man said, "we know God has sent this Yolanda." Another man said, "Some people say Yolanda is man-made. I don't think that. It is allowed by God, coming here so that the people will know in that typhoon God made it and the people will know there is a living God and we need God." This is not to say that they did not prepare for other typhoons, as noted previously, but that their theological explanation overrode scientific explanations rather than operating together as with explanations given by Catholic participants. Although they did not posit that human activity was potentially linked to the intensity of the typhoon, this did not stop them from thinking about the dangers of disaster risk creation and the need for disaster preparedness in the face of changing climatic hazards, meaning that this interpretation is not mutually exclusive to disaster risk reduction activities. An examination of religious subtleties between Catholics and those from Protestant denominations will demonstrate how assuming homogeneity in a Christian population will bar secular humanitarians from understanding this crucial social dynamic.

People also had relationships with the international humanitarian organisations that responded to Haiyan. People affected by Haiyan mostly mentioned the basic similarities between international organisations that were faith-based and secular, mainly to make a contrast to national organisations. They both constructed ideas around the characteristics of secular and FBOs but also allowed that there were exceptions to these. The majority felt that national faith-affiliated groups, such as women religious, were closest to them and their needs. The data should not be over-interpreted to force a position of differentiated secularity and this section means to recognise the interweaving and not mutually exclusive nature of secular and religious positions, as well as the times in which these positions were superseded by other concerns. While some people said that FBOs assisted because "it's from their heart," it was also added by a few that they felt secular organisations also gave from their hearts meaning that there was no consistent difference in this way. One person said about secular organisations, "If their motive is to help us with the good of everybody, then it's fine." While it was said that secular organisations mainly did distribution without much human interaction and FBOs were more focused on human interaction, some noted that there had been secular organisations that would "give words of encouragement" as they put it. While they still maintained that this was largely the preserve of the national FBOs, it was not an action that was solely given by them. There was one fundamental issue that arose. While not echoed by all, there was one woman who summarised the position felt by several research participants,

> For me, everybody of us has faith. But with an emergency like Yolanda, we forgot our faith. And any NGO that comes to our barangay, we don't mind what kind of religion is that who came to our barangay. The most important is the help, the assistance which we need. Which is given to us. We forget our faith, even what religion is that. The important is the help they give to us.

This example shows the mutability of people's position in the emergency period when they need assistance. The participants did not lose their religious identity after disaster, but in this scenario, and the fact that they need assistance, means that they will put faith, their own and that of NGOs, to the side.

Religion as practice: ritual and quotidian practice

Geertz' work in the 1960s postulated that religion is a "cultural system." Within this cultural system, ritual is one of the most powerful elements that brings people together in the collective. Geertz points to the nature of religious ritual as a "drawing near, not a standing back" (Geertz 1993, p. 116) to demonstrate that ritual is not something observed from the outside by the believer but something that draws them in and to which they fully partici- pate. Some of the very earliest images broadcast around the world after the earthquake hit Haiti in 2010 were the gatherings of survivors, sometimes in their hundreds, in ruined churches to collectively sing hymns and pray. The hypothesis that ritual is more than a merely superficial construct is shown in the immediate reaction of the Haitian people who gathered together to perform the religious rituals they had followed before the disaster. The Haitian survivors were not singing hymns as a mere process in a religious ceremony but were inspired to sing out as part of their physical and mental participation in the collective healing process of the religious ritual. Else- where, Falk reports how merit-making ceremonies rapidly increased after the Indian Ocean tsunami in 2004 so that Buddhist survivors could transfer merit to their dead family members (Falk 2014, p. 116). Likewise, the ritual practice of prayer has been shown by several studies to aid resilience to trauma and disasters (for example, Ai *et al.* 2005; Fernando and Hebert 2011). Religion has an inbuilt coping mechanism for trauma survivors and thus in the post-disaster context is one of the more important social institu- tions. One might assume that disaster would incur a loss of religious faith, but people turn to religion once again, even after such a catastrophe. To turn away from religion at that point would only compound their sense of loss and chaos. Instead, by turning to religion, they had some sense of order and reassurance.

For people affected by Haiyan, the important rituals encountered were prayer (particularly, the Rosary) and Mass (and Mass during Saints' days fiestas and Christmas and Holy Week in particular). Prayer was the constant undercurrent of all focus groups. A woman, who had sheltered under her bed with her children, as her home was ripped apart by the winds around them, most vividly described the image. She said in that moment she prayed with her children. It is a hardwired and deep-seated response that recog- nises the point at which nothing more can be physically done to protect your safety by your own means. Instead, there is a turn to the divine. Like- wise, the familiarity of religious ritual in the form of Christmas festivities was particularly important. These religious celebrations with their associ- ated rituals help people draw together and fully participate in the collective cultural system that is their religion. In one example, from a small village whose chapel had been severely damaged by the typhoon, they focused their initial efforts on building a temporary wooden chapel, just in front of their former concrete chapel, as they were able to get this ready in time for Christmas (which was a month and a half after the typhoon). While they were still working as a community to raise funds to rebuild their concrete chapel, they were still using this wooden chapel at the time of this research, 16 months later.

A notable example of the positive effects for an organisation of taking religious ritual into account is the Tzu Chi Foundation. Although a Buddhist organisation, they donated a large sum to rebuild the Santo Nino Church in downtown Tacloban, which is iconic in the local area. Their popularity among the population is incredibly high and this act was particularly popular. Other recent research has demonstrated much popular support for Tzu Chi in the Philippines, with Catholic Filipinos finding self-fulfilment in the organisation (Lau and Cornelio 2015) and beneficiaries frequently citing it as the most helpful organisation with the cultivation of a "philosophy of love and care for their beneficiaries . . . through early and sustained presence on the ground" (Corpus *et al.* 2015, pp. 26, 55).

Conclusion

The chapter has reviewed religious responses to disaster, disaster risk, and vulnerability in the Visayan region of the Philippines and following the impacts of Typhoon Haiyan. It started with a review of the cultural responses to disaster in the Philippines and the ways in which other researchers have pinpointed the role of religion for Filipinos in disaster. This demonstrated that religion is undoubtedly a significant part of Filipino resilience, but it also highlighted a few contested areas such as fatalistic responses to disaster risk prompted by religious interpretations. After Haiyan, this research found that people did not have a binary view of what was out of their control as part of God's plan and what was within their control as active agents living in a place facing many hazards. While seemingly contradictory, it was not inconsistent for research participants to hold both perspectives at the same time.

Through the use of Woodhead's concepts of religion, several key elements of religion in disaster were highlighted, in conjunction with reflections on some of the most classic theories from the sociology of religion. It shows that response to disaster has always been at the core of much theorising about religion in society and that the application of these theories from the sociology of religion remains relevant for nuancing the contemporary fields of humanitarian and disaster studies. In this research their application primarily underlined the significance of religion in community relations, particularly environmental stewardship, meaning making of the disaster, and the place of ritual, particularly prayer.

Bibliography

Abinales, M., 2003. In Times of Affliction: God and Preparedness are our Protection. *Philippine Sociological Review*, 52, 154–162.

Ai, A.L., Tice, T.N., Peterson, C., and Huang, B., 2005. Prayers, Spiritual Support, and Positive Attitudes in Coping with the September 11 National Crisis. *Journal of Personality*, 73 (3), 763–792.

Alatas, S.F., and Sinha, V., 2017. *Sociological Theory Beyond the Canon*. London: Palgrave Macmillan.

Aldrovandi, C., 2014. *Apocalyptic Movements in Contemporary Politics: Christian and Jewish Zionism*. Basingstoke: Palgrave Macmillan.

Almazan, J.U., Cruz, J.P., Alamri, M.S., Alotaibi, J.S.M., Albougami, A.S.B., Gravoso, R., Abocejo, F., Allen, K., and Bishwajit, G., 2018. Predicting Patterns of Disaster-related Resiliency Among Older Adult Typhoon Haiyan Survivors. *Geriatric Nursing*, 39 (6), 629–634.

Are We Losing Faith? An Invitation to the Sociology of Religion in the Philippines. *Social Studies Corner* (blog). https://socialstudiescorner.wordpress.com/2014/11/20/are-we-losing-faith-an-invitation-to-the-sociology-of-religion-in-the-philippines/.

Aten, J.D., Ayers, J., Boan, D., Chadburn, O., Haw, S., Howard, P., Ingram, T., Kalantzis, G., Koach, L., MacMillan, C., Nisley, B., Integral Alliance, and Martinson, D., 2015. *A Call to Commitment and Partnership: A World Evangelical Alliance Brief on the Evangelical Community and Humanitarian Development*. World Evangelical Alliance.

Bankoff, G., 2003. *Cultures of Disaster: Society and Natural Hazard in the Philippines*. London: RoutledgeCurzon.

Bankoff, G. 2004. In the Eye of the Storm: The Social Construction of the Forces of Nature and the Climatic and Seismic Construction of God in the Philippines. *Journal of Southeast Asian Studies*, 35 (1), 91–111.

Bankoff, G., 2007. Living with Risk; Coping with Disasters: Hazard as a Frequent Life Experience in the Philippines. *Education About Asia*, 12 (2), 26–29.

Bankoff, G., 2015. "Lahat para sa lahat" (Everything to Everybody): Consensual Leadership, Social Capital and Disaster Risk Reduction in a Filipino Community. *Disaster Prevention and Management: An International Journal*, 24 (4), 430–447.

Bankoff, G., Cannon, T., Kruger, F., and Schipper, E.L.F., 2015. Introduction: Exploring the Links Between Cultures and Disasters. *In:* G. Bankoff, T. Cannon, F. Kruger, B. Orlowski, and E.L.F. Schipper, eds. *Cultures and Disasters: Understanding Cultural Framings in Disaster Risk Reduction*. Abingdon: Routledge.

Barmania, S., 2014. Typhoon Haiyan Recovery: Progress and Challenges. *The Lancet* 383 (April): 1197–99.

Berger, P., 1967. *The Sacred Canopy: Elements of a Sociological Theory of Religion*. Anchor Books.

Bollettino, V., Alcayna, T., Enriquez, K., and Vinck, P., 2018. *Perceptions of Disaster Resilience and Preparedness in the Philippines | Harvard Humanitarian Initiative*. Cambridge, MA: Harvard Humanitarian Initiative.

Browne, K.E., 2015. *Standing in the Need: Culture, Comfort, and Coming Home After Katrina*. Austin: University of Texas Press.

Browne, K.E., and Olson, L., 2019. *Building Cultures of Preparedness: A Report for the Emergency Management Higher Education Community*. Washingtion, DC: The U.S. Federal Emergency Management Agency (FEMA).

Buckley, D., 2017. *Faithful to Secularism: The Religious Politics of Democracy in Ireland, Senegal, and the Philippines*. 1st ed. New York City: Columbia University Press.

Cannon, T., Schipper, L., Bankoff, G., and Kruger, F., 2014. *World Disasters Report: Focus on Culture and Risk*. Geneva: International Federation of Red Cross and Red Crescent Societies.

Carandang, Ma.L.A., 1996. *Pakikipagkapwa-Damdamin: Accompanying Survivors of Disaster*. Makati City: Bookmark, Inc.

Cardinal Tagle, H.E.L.A.G., 2015. *FULL TEXT: Cardinal Tagle's Speech After Pope Mass at Cathedral* [online]. Available from: www.gmanetwork.com/news/story/406602/news/nation/full-text-cardinal-tagle-s-speech-after-pope-mass-at-cathedral [Accessed 20 January 2015].

Cheema, A.R., Scheyvens, R., Glavovic, B., and Imran, M., 2014. Unnoticed but Important: Revealing the Hidden Contribution of Community-Based Religious Institution of the Mosque in Disasters. *Natural Hazards*, 71 (3), 2207–2229.

Cherry, K.E., Sampson, L., Galea, S., Marks, L.D., Stanko, K.E., Nezat, P.F., and Baudoin, K.H., 2018. Spirituality, Humor, and Resilience After Natural and Technological Disasters. *Journal of Nursing Scholarship*.

Clarke, G., and Jennings, M., eds., 2008. *Development, Civil Society and Faith-Based Organisations: Bridging the Sacred and the Secular*. Basingstoke: Palgrave Macmillan.

Cornelio, J.S., 2014. Popular Religion and the Turn to Everyday Authenticity: Reflections on the Contemporary Study of Philippine Catholicism. *Philippine Studies: Historical and Ethnographic Viewpoints*, 62 (3), 471–500.

Cornelio, J.S., and Sapitula, M.V.J., 2015. Are We Losing Faith? An Invitation to the Sociology of Religion in the Philippines. *Social Studies Corner.*

Corpus, O.J., Flores, J.M., and Combinido, P., 2015. *Obliged to be Grateful: How Local Communities Experienced Humanitarian Actors in the Haiyan Response*. Woking: Plan International.

Crittenden, K.S., and Rodolfo, K.S., 2002. Bacolor Town and Pinatubo Volcano, Philippines: Coping with Recurrent Lahar Disaster. *In:* R. Torrence and J. Grattan, eds. *Natural Disasters and Cultural Change*. London: Routledge.

Darcy, J., Leonardi E., Robitaille P., Monzanal M., and Gandin J., n.d. Real-Time Evaluation of UNICEF's Humanitarian Response to Typhoon Haiyan in the Philippines. New York: UNICEF. Accessed July 15, 2015. http://www.alnap.org/resource/12697.

de la Cruz, G., 2015. How Vulnerable Is Manila to Earthquakes? [online]. *Rappler*. Available from: www.rappler.com/move-ph/issues/disasters/knowledge-base/76464-how-vulnerable-manila-earthquakes [Accessed 29 July 2015].

Durkheim, E., 1915. *The Elementary Forms of the Religious Life*. London: George Allen & Unwin Ltd.

Esteban, Audrey O. 2015. "Philippines Typhoon Appeal: Contribution to Change Study." London: Disasters Emergency Committee; Ateneo de Manila University School of Government.

Falk, M.L., 2014. *Post-Tsunami Recovery in Thailand: Socio-cultural Responses.* Abingdon, New York.

Featherstone, A., 2014. *Missed Again: Making Space for Partnership in the Typhoon Haiyan Response.* London: Christian Aid; CAFOD; Oxfam GB; Tearfund; Action Aid.

Featherstone, A., 2015. *Keeping the Faith: The Role of Faith Leaders in the Ebola Response.* London; Birmingham; Teddington: Christian Aid; CAFOD; Tearfund; Islamic Relief Worldwide.

Fernando, D.M., and Hebert, B.B., 2011. Resiliency and Recovery: Lessons From the Asian Tsunami and Hurricane Katrina. *Journal of Multicultural Counseling and Development*, 39 (1), 2–13.

Fiddian-Qasmiyeh, E., and Ager, A., 2013. *Local Faith Communities and the Promotion of Resilience in Humanitarian Situations: A Scoping Study.* Oxford: Joint Learning Initiative on Faith and Local Communities and RSC Working Paper.

Field, J., 2016. A Culture Clash? Exploring 'Appropriateness' and 'Relevance' in the Response to Typhoon Haiyan/Yolanda. *In:* F. Espada, ed. *Essays on Humanitarian Effectiveness.* London: Humanitarian Affairs Team, Save the Children & Humanitarian and Conflict Response Institute.

Field, J., 2017. What Is Appropriate and Relevant Assistance After a Disaster? Accounting for Culture(s) in the Response to Typhoon Haiyan/Yolanda. *International Journal of Disaster Risk Reduction*, 22, 335–344.

Frazer, J.G., 2009. *The Golden Bough: A Study in Magic and Religion.* One-volume ed. Oxford: Oxford University Press.

Freud, S., 2008. *The Future of an Illusion.* London: Penguin.

Gaillard, J.C., Liamzon C.C., and Maceda, E.A., 2005. Act of Nature or Act of Man? Tracking the Root Causes of Increasing Disasters in the Philippines. *Philippine Geographical Journal* Volume 49 (Nos. 1–4).

Garcia, A., 2010. Installing Early Warning System along the Agos River in the Municipalities of Infanta and General Nakar. *In:* L. Polotan-dela Cruz, E.M. Ferrer, and Pagaduan, eds. *Building Disaster-Resilient Communities: Stories and Lessons from the Philippines.* Quezon City: University of the Philippines, College of Social Work and Community Development, 9–22.

Gaspar, Bro.K., 2014. *Mission Among the Survivors of Haiyan.*

Geertz, C., 1993. Religion as a Cultural System. *In: The Interpretation of Cultures: Selected Essays.* London: Fontana Press, 87–125.

Hearth, K., n.d. Haiyan Recovery Spurs Spiritual Growth. *Mission Network News* (blog). Accessed March 7, 2015. https://www.mnnonline.org/news/haiyan-recovery-spurs-spiritual-growth/.

Hervieu-Léger, D., 2000. *Religion as a Chain of Memory.* Cambridge: Polity Press.

Hilhorst, D., Baart, J., Haar, G. van der, and Leeftink, F.M., 2015. Is Disaster "Normal" for Indigenous People? Indigenous Knowledge and Coping Practices. *Disaster Prevention and Management: An International Journal*, 24 (4), 506–522.

Holden, W., 2015. From the Church of the Powerful to the Church of the Poor: Liberation Theology and Catholic Praxis in the Philippines. *In:* S.D. Brunn, ed. *The Changing World Religion Map: Sacred Places, Identities, Practices and Politics.* Dordrecht: Springer Netherlands, 3095–3114.

Ignacio, L.L., and Perlas, A.P., 1994. *From Victims to Survivors: Psychosocial Intervention in DIsaster Management*. Manila: UP Manila Information, Publication and Public Affairs Office (IPPAO).

IOM, 2015. IOM and the Norwegian Government Donate X-Ray Machine and Paging System to Roxas City. *Philippines Response Blog: Humanitarian Communications* (blog). http://philippineresponse.iom.int/blog/iom-and-norwegian-government-donate-x-ray-machine-and-paging-system-roxas-city.

Lau, A.L., and Cornelio, J.S., 2015. Tzu Chi and the Philanthropy of Filipino Volunteers. *Asian Journal of Social Science* 43 (4): 376–99.

Lauer, M., 2012. Oral Traditions or Situated Practices? Understanding How Indigenous Communities Respond to Environmental Disasters. *Human Organization*, 71 (2), 176–187.

Lin, J.J., and Lin, W.I., 2016. Cultural Issues in Post-disaster Reconstruction: The Case of Typhoon Morakot in Taiwan. *Disasters*, 40 (4), 668–692.

Luna, E.M., 2003. Endogenous System of Response to River Flooding as a Disaster Subculture: A Case Study of Bula, Camarines Sur. *Philippine Sociological Review*, 51.

Luna, E.M., 2006. Transforming the Vulnerabilities, Empowering the Vulnerable: Framework on Community Development for Disaster Risk Reduction in the Philippines. *In: Conference on Disaster Management Through Regional Cooperation, Association of Southeast Asia Institutions of Higher Learning*. Presented at the Conference on Disaster Management Through Regional Cooperation, Association of Southeast Asia Institutions of Higher Learning, University of Indonesia, Jakarta.

Magalang, M.R., 2010. Mainstreaming Disaster Risk Reduction and Climate Change Adaptation in Mandatory Planning and Budgeting Processes of Barangays: A Case Study on Building Disaster Resilient Communities in Marinduque. *In: Building Disaster-resilient Communities: Stories and Lessons from the Philippines*. Quezon City: University of the Philippines, College of Social Work and Community Development, 67–90.

Malinowski, B., 1974. *Magic, Science and Religion, and Other Essays*. London: Souvenir Press.

Mangarin, D.C., Sr.F.R., 2013. *Faith-Based Organizing Processes and Strategies in Disaster Affected Community: The Case of Barangay Pinaglapatan, Infanta, Quezon*. Master's Thesis. College of Social Work and Community Development, University of the Philippines, Quezon City.

Martin, M., 2013. Faith Sustains Filipinos after Typhoon Haiyan. *Our Sunday Visitor Catholic Publishing Company*, November 21, 2013. https://www.osv.com/OSVNewsweekly/InFocus/Article/TabId/721/ArtMID/13629/ArticleID/13456/Faith-sustains-Filipinos-after-Typhoon-Haiyan.aspx.

Mercado, L.N., ed., 2000. *Filipino Popular Devotions: The Interior Dialogue Between Traditional Religion & Christianity*. Manila: Logos Publications, Inc.

Mercer, J., Kelman, I., Suchet-Pearson, S., and Lloyd, K., 2009. Integrating Indigenous and Scientific Knowledge Bases for Disaster Risk Reduction in Papua New Guinea. *Geografiska Annaler: Series B, Human Geography*, 91 (2), 157–183.

Moreno, A.F., 2006. *Church, State, and Civil Society in Postauthoritarian Philippines: Narratives of Engaged Citizenship*. Quezon City: Ateneo de Manila University Press.

O'Connell, E.P., Abbott, R.P., and White, R.S., 2017. Religious Struggles After Typhoon Haiyan: A Case Study from Bantayan Island. *Disaster Prevention and Management: An International Journal*, 26 (3), 330–347.

Pope Francis. 2015a. "FULL TEXT: Pope Francis' Homily, Holy Mass in Tacloban." *Rappler*. January 17, 2015. http://www.rappler.com/specials/pope-francis-ph/81106-full-text-pope-francis-homily-tacloban.

———. 2015b. "ENCYCLICAL LETTER LAUDATO SI' OF THE HOLY FATHER FRANCIS ON CARE FOR OUR COMMON HOME," May 24, 2015. http://w2.vatican.va/content/francesco/en/encyclicals/documents/papa-francesco_20150524_enciclica-laudato-si.html.

Quirino, M., 2014. A Fisherman's Prayer. *Rappler*, November 23, 2014. http://www.rappler.com/move-ph/issues/disasters/recovery/75594-fisherman-prayer.

Sadowski, D., 2014. Philippine Cardinal: Haiyan Recovery Can Show World a United Church. *Catholic News Service*, February 3, 2014. http://www.catholicnews.com/data/stories/cns/1400469.htm.

Sapitula, M.V.J., 2015. Religious Pluralism and Sociological Engagement: Reflections of a Young Sociologist from the Philippines. *ISA e Symposium for Sociology*, 14.

Schipper, E.L.F., 2015. Religion and Belief Systems: Drivers of Vulnerability, Entry Points for Resilience Building? *In:* G. Bankoff, T. Cannon, F. Kruger, B. Orlowski, and E.L.F. Schipper, eds. *Cultures and Disasters: Understanding Cultural Framings in Disaster Risk Reduction*. Abingdon: Routledge.

Sison, S., 2014. The Problem with Filipino Resilience [online]. *Rappler*. Available from: www.rappler.com/move-ph/ispeak/73433-problem-filipino-resilience [Accessed 12 June 2015].

Thomson Reuters, 2015. Pope Francis Holds Mass in Typhoon-Ravaged Tacloban in Philippines. January 17, 2015. http://www.cbc.ca/news/world/pope-francis-holds-mass-in-typhoon-ravaged-tacloban-in-philippines-1.2916531.

Wilkinson, O., 2015. *Faith and Resilience After Disaster: The Case of Typhoon Haiyan*. Dublin: Misean Cara.

Wong-Fernandez, B., 1996. *Psychosocial Response of Women to Two Types of Disaster in the Philippines*. PhD Thesis. Asian Center, University of the Philippines Diliman, Quezon City.

Workman, K., 2013. Heartbreaking Photos Show Human Cost of Typhoon Haiyan. Mercury News. November 11, 2013. http://www.spundge.com/@/story/10034/.

Woodhead, L., 2011. Five Concepts of Religion. *International Review of Sociology*, 21 (1), 121–143.

Woods, L.S., 2002. *A Broken Mirror: Protestant Fundamentalism in the Philippines*. Quezon City: New Day Publishers.

4 How humanitarians experience secular dynamics in the humanitarian system

The secularity of the humanitarian system exists in norms communicated by expectations and between individuals, organisations, and disaster-affected communities. Just as we expect to see variation within the theologies of different denominations of a religion, we also see variations in how secularity is interpreted by and affects different people. Secular humanitarians therefore exhibit a wide range of interpretations of their secularity in relation to the religious beliefs and practices of others around them, including their colleagues and partner organisations. Without advocating for only one way of understanding secularity in humanitarian action, NGO staff held a relatively clear consensus that secular organisations are defined by the absence of religion in their mission and vision, they do not proselytise, religion is not to be mentioned or taboo, and respectfulness must be maintained. As conversations progressed, though, nuances in this picture emerged, and contradicted many of the views of people affected by the disaster. Two broad areas of debate are particularly representative of the issues at stake: secular humanitarians preferred efficiency whereas beneficiaries preferred interaction; and secular humanitarians believed they were better at impartiality (and neutrality to some degree) whereas beneficiaries thought they were less impartial.

These staff came from international, national, and local backgrounds. Some of them have strong religious beliefs and practices, while still contributing to the maintenance of an overall secular humanitarian system. Some of them are atheist, others agnostic. Their individual beliefs are not in question here. Instead, I interrogate their contributions to the public sphere of the secular humanitarian system. This chapter explores, first, some of the main secular parameters as defined by humanitarian staff and, second, how these demonstrate secular boundary-making in the humanitarian system.

Characterising a secular approach in the Haiyan response

No proselytising

The most immediate and easily identifiable characteristic is that secular NGOs do not proselytise. This was a sentiment echoed particularly by national staff. One national staff member for an international organisation said, "You are free to practice whatever, but you cannot preach your faith. Filipinos understand that." Another national staff member from a national organisation said, "We support [an international FBO], but we are very conscious they should not proselytise. But there are also groups that proselytise and we do not want [that]." International staff did not state this outright as much, perhaps because it is such a given within the NGO community, but would engage with the problems that proselytisation can engender. One staff member in a European headquarters who had engaged with the Haiyan response noted,

> When you preach your own beliefs, even if it is not about faith, but just your beliefs, it's risky, because what you see is that they don't trust the NGOs. Because you are overruling the local practices, like the medicine man and the shaman. I think that's always a challenge for whatever organisation you are from.

This demonstrates flexibility around the type of "belief" that is being propagated in proselytisation and recognition that it is not just religious beliefs that can be imposed.

Organisational mission and vision

Another characterisation that is more widely known from the literature (Thaut 2009) is that an organisation's mission and vision will make it clear if they are secular or not. Several respondents confirmed that the organisational orientation was an indicator of secularity. A national staff member for an international NGO explained that your orientation once you start at the organisation clearly states that the organisation is non-religious, saying, "once you are in you accept that fact." Another said that they follow the vision and mission of the organisation agreeing "it's more organisational in structure than personal." International staff, however, were more concerned with the nuances of this organisational identity. Several noted that they relied on this organisational identity as the reason why they could not rebuild churches that had been damaged by the typhoon. The humanitarian principles were very much part of a secular identity in organisational mission and vision. An international staff member with a secular organisation explained that impartiality is "fundamental for our identity." This staff member thought that impartiality helped all staff members as "a reminder that we all come with our own baggage and perceptions . . . it serves our teams quite well and helps them confront the pressures of giving assistance to people who aren't qualified." Otherwise, the position was that secularity was found more concretely in the mandate of the organisation with one international staff member working for an international NGO notably describing the mandate as translating to them being a "purely technical organisation." In this instance, secularity meant a technical focus. Others noted that secularity is therefore clearer at the headquarters where the mandate of the organisation is shaped.

There was equally the comprehension, however, that many organisations, although faith-based in name, acted in a way that was concomitant with this secular ideal of impartiality. For example, national government staff commented on their experiences with FBOs saying that they gave for the "common good." Notably, an international staff member for a FBO said that a "non-negotiable" value of the organisation was impartiality and that they worked with a "secular set of values, derived from a biblical perspective." Many FBO respondents were keen to make it clear that the humanitarian principles were absolutely central to their work, even explaining how theological ideas were interpreted in the light of the principles rather than vice versa.

Mostly, national staff in the Philippines were happy to work within these secular frameworks. Most commonly among national staff, there was a sense that one's individual values should be kept private and that the organisational values were primary in operations, confirming the privatisation of religion that is a hallmark of a secular public space. One said that at first it was "a little bit hard to be flexible with how the [international organisation] thinks" in terms of the secular and religious, but that they had got used to it. Another staff member went as far as saying, "you think of yourself as an [international organisation] national, rather than Filipino." They said that this then made it difficult when they had to deal with religious structures. They said, "You have to respect their [churches'] views, while saying these are our [organisational] views." Ultimately, these staff members had learned how to operate in the international secular sphere and were happy to work in a culturally sensitive manner with others, but with the proviso that they were acting as their organisation rather than their personal position. National staff would recount how they were sensitive to the situation, explaining that when there were just Filipino staff around, they would pray (before meetings and at group events, for example), but when international staff were present, they would not pray. A particular national staff member who noted this behaviour said that they viewed it as a "positive, as it shows we respect other religions." This shows that the respect is not just for other religions but also secularity and those of no faith. From one international staff member's perspective, the local staff maintain the traditional in their life, but go with the international at work.

Yet there were some difficulties of this public/private divide for staff. National staff members working for an international organisation reported that they had some difficulties reconciling their faith position with that of their organisation, particularly on issues around reproductive health. It was even reported that some staff members had been asked not to go to mass because they were known to work for an organisation that endorsed certain values on reproductive health. New legislation was implemented on reproductive health in the Philippines in 2013 (Congress of the Philippines 2013) and this is a somewhat controversial topic, yet it is interesting to note the extent to which a person's private religious practice can be influenced by their employment in a secular organisation. It is not the case that secular organisations alone would advocate for certain reproductive rights, but the dominant narrative takes a position of the Church's values against secularised reproductive rights and the secular-religious tension nationally has been replicated in tensions for national staff in international secular organisations.

Religion as taboo

The secular culture within organisations was also demonstrated by a reluctance to even mention or engage with faith and religion, directly relating to Ager and Ager's specification of the marginalisation of religion in the humanitarian system as a sign of secularity. An international staff member noted, "a lot of organisations avoid talking about it." In other ways, however, religion was not so much taboo as just not included and not seen as important or necessary in the conversation. Staff would talk about it if it came up, but in most cases, as another international staff member put it, "Our programme was around cash . . . so religion wasn't involved in this conversation." Here, it was clear that there were two main reasons behind reluctance to speak of faith or religion. While some staff talked about not mentioning faith or religion because of organisational identity (e.g., from one international staff member, "Most organisations have their own mandate, which says independence and neutrality etc. Religion does not come into the picture at all. They do not talk about religion at all"), others focused on the programming aspects (e.g., from another international staff member, "Our programme wasn't religious in nature at all, there were no religious connotations"). This absence of discussion about religion or faith was reported on positively, as a sign of correctly functioning humanitarianism rather than an absence of reflection.

For national staff members, this taboo translated more into the acceptance of humanitarian rules. National staff from both secular and faith-based organisations confirmed that they never spoke about religion and that it was not something they would ever ask about in needs assessments. National staff members said, "If staff members are very religious, they would rather not mention it because there is such a mix of faiths here . . . Muslim, Iglesia Ni Cristo. . . . They understand why it's best not to mention it." Another national staff member affirmed,

> There are not really any questions involved with faith . . . we're very aware and staff are oriented not to talk about faith and not to talk about religion. Even in our implementation and processes, there is no mention of religion. . . . We are bound with our agreement in the community that our work is humanitarian and not on faith.

There were also a few staff that mentioned how this lack of discussion of faith and religion could be an impediment. One international staff member from an FBO noted

> With secular partners it's always about the humanitarian principles. It must not be about faith. It might be easier to get access to faith base because they already trust you as [an FBO]. If the whole thing is not an issue, you can just focus on the humanitarian work. You don't have to be so considerate!

From this staff member's perspective, being able to talk about faith makes it "not an issue," whereas not talking about it means that people sidestep around an issue. Another international staff member noted that there is a question around language, with some dismissive language used and a certain fear around using terms like religious mainstreaming even if it is something that happens in reality. This staff member highlighted a problematic aspect to this fear saying, "There's a perception that 'religion' will be troublesome, but all would say they try to be culturally sensitive." The question here is how actors can be culturally sensitive if they will not talk about religion.

Some secular organisations showed cognisance of personal faith among staff members. One example had their offices blessed to help make staff members feel comfortable in the physical space in which they worked. Secular, international staff members in secular operations also noted much personal negotiation with faith. One said that they were frequently asked if they were Catholic and, in order to get out of the question, they would say they had been to Catholic school without mentioning that they would not identify as Catholic otherwise. This was mentioned as a common exit strategy from such conversations for several international staff members. In interactions between international and national staff, it was often mentioned that international staff had been invited to mass or to pray before a meal shared together outside of work, for example. This was bringing the international staff member into a private space of faith, or at least a space separated from the secular work environment. Most staff members reported that this went smoothly and that if anyone felt the secular staff member did not want to cross a boundary (in one example, attending a wake), then religious staff members had understood.

There were only a couple of examples where international, secular staff members explained that they struggled to be around religion. One staff member said that as an atheist it could be particularly difficult. Even in a secular organisation, the country context often overrode this secularity and, particularly in shared accommodation provided by the organisation, religious practice would be ever present. National staff frequently confirmed the cultural divide between expats and themselves. This was something that happened in both secular and faith-based organisations – the main difference was whether they were international or not. They said that they spoke about it frequently between themselves. National staff members said they clearly knew when international staff were not practicing Catholics. One said that they would prefer for international staff members to admit that they are non-practising than say they are Catholic and then not go to mass with them on Sunday or not act it in other ways. On the other hand, however, international staff explained that it would be a hindrance for them to openly say that they were agnostic or atheist, just as some staff would not be open about their sexualities, as it would be frowned upon and potentially a hindrance to interactions with others. At this personal level, there was a complex interaction of half-truths and awareness of each other's perceptions that were navigated between secular and religious staff in organisations.

The international secularised humanitarian community is in line with the secularised Filipino government officially. However, there were several cases in which the definition of secular between these two groups was questioned. An academic noted that the definition of secularity is different in the Philippines. For example, DepEd schools are officially the secular state schools, but they teach quite a lot of religious education, with religious and secular divides carefully negotiated in the Philippines (Buckley 2017). Likewise, officially the government would not build churches, yet it was noted that they had been involved in such rebuilding projects in the typhoon-affected areas especially in the build up to the Pope's January 2015 visit. Secular international staff noted how they felt the religious orientation of government officials made them slightly uncomfortable, for example, when they were asked to engage in long prayer sessions or asked about their own faith. One noted that it could be "awkward," "made it harder to connect with people," and "closed the door to further conversation." National staff would talk about their relationship with the international secularised system.

Respectfulness

Respect was a central term used by most. FBOs reported that more secular organisations were interested in working with them and secular organisations reported mostly positive experiences in working with FBOs. Many of the examples cited in the previous sections show staff members negotiating religious and secular tensions by applying their respectfulness to others. Being respectful is a highly pragmatic decision. One national staff member for an international organisation said, "It's mandatory to be open to diversity and respectful." National staff in one secular INGO emphasised that it was important to respect other religions, one of the reasons why they did not pray when international staff were around. Another national staff member described their experience of working with international organisations and in the cluster system. They said, "They have respect and recognition in the cultures and everyone respects each other." There were examples cited (mainly from the FBO perspective) in which secular organisations had not been as respectful as perhaps some people would have wanted, but here the line between respect and abiding by certain principles is thin. Respect was also tested, according to some secular staff. One international staff member said, "it's ok to be faith-based and have half an hour of prayer, but it shouldn't influence every aspect of the work," noting that they had attended emergency preparedness trainings that were more about prayer and spiritual formation than about practical advice for preparedness. Certainly, respect can be a nebulous concept, applied as and when it suits with a certain power differential in who this "respectfulness" served, but from these interviews it was seen to be a commonly identifiable characteristic of a secular approach to interacting with religion in humanitarian action.

Respectfulness or "cultural sensitivity" in general often became a burden for national and local staff over international staff. One international staff member said that at the beginning of an emergency you should use your national staff members to do all the meetings with the local and national government structures so the response is not just perceived as the internationals taking over. Another said that things that work for locals, for example talking about religion with beneficiaries, would not work for internationals as it might "create arguments and be strange." The onus was on the national staff therefore. As one national staff member said, it is for them to "orient the expat." Another said, "It's the local staff that provide the context and the localisation of the expat expertise. So that means it's more respectful." Yet another said, "Of course the expats rely on the local staff." National staff said that there had been adaptations when differences of opinion were found. For example, one national staff member explained that, "sometimes there are some apprehensions because people [internationals] think they are good at doing this, but then there are some discussions [with the local staff], and it adapts. So, the mid-management staff are nationals so they can translate." It was often the role of the national staff to act as cultural translators in this way. Some staff felt empowered by this.

The main problem, however, was that the local knowledge of national staff gained during their field visits was not captured very well by organisations meaning that the knowledge was not fed into planning or adaptation of programmes as well as it could be. This was local level firefighting without feedback mechanisms. The international staff were not aware of many of these issues. It may not be necessary for them to know or it may be too much of an extra burden for local staff to do more reporting, but it was notable that local staff were fully aware how much they were relied on to bridge cultural divides, such as those with secular and religious dynamics. As one national staff member said, "Yes, pressure is put on national staff to take the heat." Another said there is a "burden with local staff in all emergencies because they are the ones talking directly with the people." They said in one example there had been some problems with assistance and "the people [beneficiaries] were crying and the Filipino staff had to be the buffer." An international staff member said, "With local staff, we often underestimate the pressure they are under." One national staff member explained this pressure saying that the problem as a local is that you want to please everyone, but you have to prioritise the vulnerable ones. A Filipino academic interviewed, who was also linked to the response, noted that Filipino staff working in secular organisations do not want to be flagged or marked as highly religious, so they practice self-censorship. They might engage in conversations about religion with beneficiaries, but they would not relate this to internationals higher up, hence their lack of feedback from field visits and the reality that respectfulness becomes limited to only what international staff immediately perceive as an issue. Some thought that one of the positives to note was that religion did not have a great impact on their work, if at all, in comparison to other countries where it has a greater impact. One international staff member said that they had not really felt the impact of religion on programming. They had seen it a bit during the Christmas period and said that their overall impression was that Filipinos were religious people, but it was not overt and did not include proselytising. They said, "It's private but social, as long as you're not overstepping the bounds." While a lot of cultural knowledge is not gathered, the lack of reporting also allows a freedom for local staff to operate without unnecessary restrictions. This means that strictly secular organisations can have staff members who frequently engage in prayer, ritual, and religious conversation with beneficiaries, even if the organisation is not officially aware of it. Although this is only the case with a few national staff members interviewed, a few said that they had regularly brought religion into their conversations, one even did this purposefully as they came from an evangelical denomination, although they were aware they could be fired for this. Some FBOs noted that they had had to deal with such "misunderstandings" with inexperienced field workers, as it was put by one international staff member, about beneficiaries needing to display Christian behaviour in order to receive assistance. Secular organisations gave no indication that they were aware this might happen.

Notably, a woman from the affected community expressed feelings of respectfulness for the organisations too, noting that they knew that they might not understand affected people's religiosity but respect was the way forward – the "beneficiaries" want to be culturally sensitive to the organisations from abroad. She said,

> they [the church] are the leaders, and people look at them, and they serve as our models. Setting politics aside, we still look to them for spiritual upliftment. There may be awkwardness to tell this to other [FB and secular] organisations but there is also respect. Trying to respect what they believe. They have their priorities as well.

This nuanced position explains much of the moral background to humanitarian work that is often debated. There are those who see an almost faith-like drive in humanitarians to help others (Wilkinson 2014). This woman has indicated how these quite conceptual debates around humanitarian imperatives for action can be interpreted on the ground by beneficiaries. As a man in another community summed it up, secular and FBOs are all trying to help the affected people and in that way they are fundamentally similar, while also maintaining their differences. This demonstrates that secular values are mostly felt positively while still showing that, over the course of this chapter, secular values have an impact, are perceived by communities, and are not neutral or non-existent.

"Give and goodbye!": efficiency over interaction?

One of the values that has been associated in particular with the increase in humanitarian action worldwide is that humanitarianism must use the most efficient approach in comparison to alternatives (ALNAP 2006, p. 44). NGO staff I spoke with said that secular organisations were especially efficient. A different and competing perspective emerged, however, in conversations with affected people who had experienced NGO assistance: they described secular organisations as those that stayed only for a short period of time, had little interaction with them, and focused on the material alone. The latter viewpoint will be addressed first.

Research participants from the affected population wanted more than just material goods: they wanted human and social interaction and support as well. A common critique concerned this lack of support and it was interpreted as a secular characteristic. People said things like: "some of the organisations just come for a day and then they go out"; "one time help and then no more!"; and "[they] came here only once. Once in a blue moon!". One woman summed up this approach as "give and goodbye!". There was a strong link in participants' minds between secular organisations and one-off, materially-based distributions, with lists and schedules. This was evident in all my discussions with disaster-affected people, in all areas, and among both Catholic and evangelical denominations.

The short timelines and brief interactions of secular organisations often were contrasted with those of faith-based organisations that stayed for longer. One respondent said, "they [other organisations] are gone already. One time only. But the [local faith-based organisation] always come back. They stay a number of days to follow up. A few days, to say 'how are you?'". One thing to note in these examples is that the organisations mentioned were those that had stronger ties to the area as local organisations, explaining why they were willing to stay for the longer term. Mostly, the qualitative difference expressed by participants centred on the encouragement and support gained even from someone visiting who simply asked "how are you?". This begins to demonstrate that the method of interaction with organisations frequently was crucial in people's judgements. Just as international secular organisations were characterised as focusing on lists and schedules, the local faith-based organisations were characterised by their regular visits and "how are yous?".

One woman, a Catholic and a teacher, summed up a lot of what was said across all the discussions:

> The non-faith-based is more on the material things. But those faith-based, aside from the physiological things that they provide, shelter,

food, clothing, what matters most is the spiritual achievement; it is more on the holistic human aspect. It tries to consider. Those things are just the material things. We can live with very little of that. What matters most is faith. . . . So, for the faith-based, it is more holistic, and more human at that. Considering man does not live by bread alone.

This was the contrast between organisations that concentrated on the material alone and others that included these more "holistic" aspects. People appreciated organisations that were involved in other forms of encouragement, such as blessings, counselling sessions, debriefings, prayers, spiritual formations, and other psychosocial activities. One man said, "When it's not done with words this is how they do it: Oh, you are so hungry? This is your food. . . . [We] do not feel good about that. [We] appreciate when people speak about things, words of encouragement." The impression of international NGOs from disaster-affected people was of a highly impersonal encounter, which is in comparison with the communal and interpersonal nature of relationships in the disaster-affected communities themselves, even if those interpersonal relationships are not always straightforward themselves and have been shifting over the last few decades.

Significantly, the background faith of the organisation was not always important; what was significant was that some organisations focused on impersonal lines and distributions, whereas others offered encouragement, such as a prayer. A Buddhist NGO, Tzu Chi, received particular praise from the people I spoke to in this regard: a Buddhist prayer always prefaced its work and people appreciated this time for peace and the provision of a meditative space, even though they were not of the same religion and had no intention of converting. In research with Sahrawi refugees in the Western Sahara region, Fiddian-Qasmiyeh (2011) saw how the secular and faith orientations of organisations were understood in more complex ways by the beneficiaries than by the secular and faith-based organisations themselves, to the extent that beneficiaries could work to optimise these organisational differences to their advantage (to achieve short- and long-term goals) by performing in secular ways for secular organisations and faith-based ways for faith-based organisations. Hence, the appreciation of Buddhist prayers by Tzu Chi could be more performative than spiritual. Echoing other research on accountability conducted after Haiyan (Ong, Flores, and Combinido, 2015), though, research participants underlined that they appreciated Tzu Chi more than others for its swift response and approach, which included this more "holistic" encouragement of the populace. They highlighted too that the background faith of the organisation (Buddhist in a broadly Catholic community) was not as important as the "holistic" approach. Participants said that they remained firm in their own beliefs, but that they could also benefit from these spaces of prayer and reflection. They assured me that they were not tempted in the slightest to pursue any further investigation of Tzu Chi's religion although other research in the Philippines has found that Tzu Chi are successfully gaining volunteers (converts) in Manila and other areas (Lau and Cornelio 2015). Tzu Chi's actions had conveyed what was broadly interpreted as a truly faith-based approach: they were one of the first to arrive on the scene, funded extensive cash-for-work clear up programs, included peaceful and meditative spaces in their distributions, *and* maintained a good degree of efficiency in their distributions. In comparison to other INGOs, they allowed for meaningful interactions with their beneficiaries whilst also maintaining perceived efficiency among the communities in which they worked.

Secular NGOs were broadly characterised as having a material focus, underlining immediate physical needs rather than anything else (psychological, spiritual, and otherwise). In general, instead of secular and faith-based divisions, respondents from affected populations separated organisations into two groups: those that give and those that encourage (and give). These definitions should be viewed through two lenses. First, there is an emphasis on shared relations in Filipino culture that attaches great worth to micro-level interactions between people (Yacat 2013). Affected people felt that some NGOs did not value micro-level interactions. Second, respondents often were religious people, involved in their church community. Local faith-based organisations, such as church-based organisations, with an underlying religious values system and deeply connected to the community, were more approachable than secular organisations. It is clear, therefore, why respondents thought of the former (the givers) as secular and the latter (the encouragers) as faith-based, which they favoured. While it may seem as though there is little to be done by international secular organisations, which are neither local nor faith-based, the findings reveal that changes in process and method to emphasise interaction may be beneficial. Even taking a possible faith bias among beneficiaries into account, secular organisations can still learn lessons from this analysis.

For international and several national NGO staff members, a focus on timely and efficient delivery of material on a large scale to meet "universal" needs (food, shelter, and water) was paramount in their response. These "universal" needs were naturally important to respondents from the affected population as well, but it does not diminish the fact that the method of delivery and interaction were points of criticism. A spotlight on efficiency created one of the biggest boundaries between NGOs and beneficiaries. In conversation, efficiency often translated to an emphasis on speed and achieving targets. Respondents interpreted this as a reaction to the pressures of the emergency environment to save lives, in comparison to development scenarios, or working through local religious structures, where such efficiency was not expected.

The other side of the efficiency debate, however, is that organisations feel the need to be more efficient, but that often they struggle to achieve efficiency when caught up in the bureaucracy of large-scale operations and partnerships with multiple and different types of actors. As much as the secular was characterised as concentrating on the efficient delivery of goods, it was also linked in respondents' minds to inefficient stagnations in delivery owing to bureaucracy. As one respondent from a secular international NGO put it, "[t]he church process for delivery is very simple, they just deliver food . . . if you are an individual that wants to help, don't do it through the humanitarian organisations." This was the intersection between the drive for efficiency and the bureaucratic culture in the secular humanitarian system.

The focus on efficiency and bureaucracy among secular organisations points to the centrality of material and tangible experience in a secular worldview. Achieving targets efficiently is central. Targets are quantifiably measured indicators of humanitarian action, denoting how much of a material thing has been given to whom. Organisations have technical foci and employ technical criteria to gauge success, showing that other principles or notions of success are truly displaced in the secular humanitarian system. Common definitions of the secular denote everything that is of this world, temporal, and material. Technical and material foci represent a secular approach in that they centre on what is important for "human flourishing" within this world (Taylor 2007, p. 20), such as material sustenance. Thus, secular humanitarianism justifies its material focus using a rationality that sees the extent of human experience happening within a tangible and material world and responds to that. In contrast, there is no opportunity or yardstick that secular organisations can utilise to determine the effectiveness of the presence of religion in people's daily lives; "spiritual achievement," as a respondent put it, also prioritises mental sustenance from non-worldly sources. These aspects of life do not make sense, therefore, or work in the light of the considerations of the secular humanitarian system.

Interactions in the field were influenced by secular boundary-making, but systems of boundary-breaking were also evidenced, revealing that secular-religious interaction is something that NGO staff navigate carefully. One of the main areas of negotiation concerned religious ceremonies, one of the main ways in which secular humanitarians interact with the religious belief and practice of disaster-affected people. Notably, ceremonies take place at ground breakings for new constructions, when items are handed over (such as a ceremony for a new fishing boat), or when moving into new shelters. As several national staff members explained, this can be about both organised religion, superstition, and animistic beliefs. For example, a priest may be present to bless the building with holy water and afterwards a chicken may be sacrificed and its blood wiped on to the foundations. Staff were divided about the level to which organisations should be involved in these ceremonies, ranging from those who did not engage at all to those who participated actively. Likewise, there were differences between those secular organisations that helped organise the blessing and accounted for any associated expenses in the miscellaneous section of budgets (related expenses were very small), and those organisations that believed it was for the community to set up, but would happily participate once arrangements were in place. As one national staff member commented on a ceremony involving the sacrifice of a chicken: "[w]e don't believe it, but if they ask for it we join. . . . If it's not destructive, then why not? That's my bench line."

Examples I encountered included blessings of boats and (re-)constructions of buildings, blessings of medical equipment donated to hospitals, blessings of office buildings for secular INGOs when it was requested by their national staff, and invitations for INGOs to participate in fiestas, including the religious mass in those fiestas. I attended one such fiesta from the invitation of a local faith-based organisation in March 2015. A mass was followed by food and dancing in the village hall and square. Secular humanitarians reported that they had been invited to fund such events – there is usually a major funder called a "hermano/a mayor" – with varying acceptances and refusals. There were none that became the major funder, but some had participated, whereas others had kept a distance.

Secular organisations were not averse to starting community, staff, or partnership meetings with prayers. Some organisations said that they always did so, led by national staff members, whereas others said that they did so if the community made a request. One national staff member who had also worked internationally pointed out that "it's about respecting the existing practices," adding that there were some international staff members who were not respectful of the time to pray, which caused some consternation. A national staff member from a secular international organisation said: "[s]o people start with a prayer, it's part of everyday life, but not glaringly or too obvious. So, faith can come in, but not religion," indicating that private, personal beliefs are momentarily accepted into the secular, humanitarian public space but that the systems of institutionalised religion, or the positions of church communities as a body, are not as welcome.

A matter that arose frequently in interviews were community members asking secular humanitarians to help rebuild churches. Most people saw this as a clear boundary in their work. The practicalities of budgetary constrictions often were noted – where a prayer costs nothing, the reconstruction of a church is significant – as were programme objectives – the initiative was designed around cash delivery or shelter construction, for instance, and the reconstruction of a church was not within the remit of the project. Mostly people viewed it as the responsibility of the church to find the funds for reconstruction. A national staff member said that she had had to clarify this to communities on several occasions. Although she clearly knew why they could not help to build a chapel, she also stressed that it "can be difficult" and you have "to be careful not to offend." There were a few exceptions, however. One was cash-for-work programming to help fix community cultural spaces such as the basketball court, the barangay hall, or the chapel. Another was when some leftover materials were provided to the community to restore cultural buildings as they wished. Yet another was when "multi-purpose" community spaces were built that the community could use as desired, including as a religious space.

Disaster-affected people offered an alternative perspective, stating that they knew organisations were not interested in funding chapel rehabilitation and mostly fundraised within the community for such work. As with Sahrawi refugees (Fiddian-Qasmiyeh 2011), performance and adherence to the perceived aims of the external organisations affected the positions of the affected population. Secular parameters acquired the upper hand because of the power dynamic that puts the giver in charge of defining needs. Participants learned to stop asking for chapel rehabilitation and instead relied on other mechanisms, including local patronage (such as the *hermano/a mayor*). In sum, most secular organisations were willing to participate in religious practices if asked to do so by beneficiaries or local staff. The evidence of the secular was apparent not in when they took part, but where they drew boundaries. Prayer is fine, but not too much. Participation in religious ceremonies is fine, but building a church is not. To this extent, the secular approach to interaction with their beneficiaries' beliefs acknowledges the existence of such beliefs but does not put any more worth in them than is strictly necessary to maintain smooth relations. This links with the theory of Ager and Ager (2015) by demonstrating one of the more subtle ways in which religion is instrumentalised so that international organisations are accepted in communities, and marginalised so that it does not take up great significance in the humanitarian response.

"Promises, promises": questions of impartiality, neutrality, and transparency

Impartiality, neutrality, and transparency also emerged in discussions to characterise the secular. Disaster-affected people I spoke to felt that secular organisations were less impartial and transparent than non-secular entities. One person lamented that these organisations had made so many "promises, promises" with little effect. One should note here that there was strong bias against politicians in the Haiyan response, and secular organisations frequently were simply placed in the same category as governmental agencies without specific reference to a differentiation between governmental and international organisations. Secular organisations often go to "barangay captains" (local-level political leaders) as a way of accessing a community (whereas faith-based organisations also go through religious leaders), but this can make them seem less neutral and impartial; people commonly believe that barangay officials will reward family and friends (Corpus *et al.* 2015, p. 9). Organisations must coordinate with the government to minimise gaps in assistance and duplication of efforts, but one of the effects of this is that they inherit the negatives associated with these governmental partners. In the Filipino context this impacted majorly on the perceived impartiality, neutrality, and transparency of NGOs in the eyes of the affected population, with some secular organisations allegedly even being banned from communities for having close political ties. Research participants trusted local religious leaders in comparison to political leaders and organisations working through these leaders gained trust and legitimacy on these grounds, leading to perceived increase in impartiality.

In contrast to the opinions of affected people who viewed secular organisations as less impartial than faith-based ones, NGO participants described secular organisations as more impartial, leading to better access to affected people. There was a general perception that a religious approach to humanitarian action might mean that not all people were assisted or that only certain denominations were served. This was the case for national and international personnel working for secular organisations. One national staff member pointed out that, "[i]f you're too involved in the religion, you're not objective." Impartiality was seen as a clear advantage to secular organisations mostly because there was no question about whether or not a certain congregation should be attended over others. As one international staff member surmised, "[i]t's easier for us to be impartial and toe the line. It can make the parameters of work clearer."

This was contradicted in examples of partnerships between secular international NGOs and secular local partners, which, in turn, would partner with local church-based organisations. By adding an extra layer of removal, a process of boundary-moving could occur, leaving the secular international NGOs satisfied with the local secular partner and the local secular partner being able to fund local faith-based organisations, which otherwise might not have been acceptable. In this way, local secular organisations can act as a form of "culture broker" (Browne 2015, p. 23), able to navigate between differing secularisms to understand both what is expected internationally and what is normal locally. Browne's (2015) conception of a culture broker comes from years of work with an affected family following Hurricane

Katrina in the United States in August 2005. She saw how many family members struggled to work with the bureaucracy of government and some aid organisations, but that one family member who was familiar with administrative procedures could help all of the others and act as a bridge between worlds. The post-Haiyan and post-Katrina cases demonstrate how cultural divergences form a barrier to those affected by a disaster, with those holding more power because of their resources, such as aid agencies and governments, failing to understand how these practices marginalise some individuals. Pressure is put on affected people to locate culture brokers that can forge inroads with respect to communication and negotiation.

The humanitarian principles provide a notable point of resonance with secularisation theses. They ground humanitarianism in a modernist, utilitarian morality that cements an internal secular rationality created for the humanitarian sphere and confirms a secular outlook based on assumptions of secular humanitarianism being universalistic (as opposed to the particularism of religion). That said, the other principles (aside from impartiality) had little resonance among research participants. In fact, humanity and independence were barely noted at all. Neutrality was mentioned, but with significant caveats about needing to coordinate with local government officials. Respondents hung on to the idea of impartiality as a forte of secular humanitarianism, but were freer with their loyalty to neutrality, stating that operations must link with politics to be effective.

Understanding secular boundary-making and -breaking

There were several examples of boundary formation in a secular approach. Boundaries were rationalised and justified, with staff noting that cultural aspects such as the rebuilding of churches were the responsibility of the community. Conversely, however, organisations were willing to fund other cultural items, such as community halls, demonstrating that their secularity ultimately dictated what was, or was not, considered as a worthy "need." Yet, boundaries could be compromised quickly, leading to complications in which secular staff would have to think creatively or bow out of interactions. Compromise was key in these situations and secular organisations and staff frequently would go far to ensure that they were accepted and were acceptable to the local people with whom they wanted to work. This demonstrates that instrumentalisation of religious practices to smooth relations can be seen from an alternative perspective in which, in fact, it aids the contextualisation of disaster response.

There were examples of when these boundaries had not been compromised, though, and cultural barriers or blockages had formed. Some said they were one reason why there was a high turnover of local staff in some organisations. Not all secular organisations came across these cultural barriers or blockages, whereas others navigated them successfully, but they do serve to illustrate times when the marginalisation of religion in humanitarian action led to mistakes.

One staff member underlined that religion only becomes an issue when you do not talk about it, while another noted the irony of secularised cultural sensitivity in which religion is seen as troublesome and something to be avoided – the underpinnings of the secular approach to humanitarian action foreshadowed problems ahead. These instances related not only to barriers or blockages but also to missed opportunities for partnerships. Affected people favoured linkages with churches owing to trustworthiness, but humanitarian actors looked to political institutions, remaining nervous of religious institutions. This is not to say that one type of institution is better than the other – in fact, an underlying current of this research affirms the value of secular and religious institutions in disaster response. Instead, this demonstrates how secular assumptions affect humanitarian decision-making following a disaster and consequently impact on beneficiaries' perceptions of secular organisations.

A dominant line of thought for secular organisations throughout was that culture and religion are elements warranting attention in development, but that the key focus of disaster response is efficiency and "universal" needs. First, this begs the question as to at what point culture and religion become relevant on the relief and development timeline. A number of authors, including Bailey and Pavanello (2009), underscore that the emergency, recovery, and development phases are hardly clear-cut. Likewise, the Haiyan response cannot be neatly categorised, as people affected by the typhoon engaged almost immediately in recovery (Hanley *et al.* 2014), the government called an end to the response earlier than expected, and many "humanitarian" organisations stayed long into the recovery phase. When should humanitarians start incorporating these perspectives? It would seem advisable to do so from the start and problematic to try to integrate them at a later stage when agendas have already been set, relationships formed, and misunderstandings developed.

Second, this prompts one to ask why cultural and religious issues are not seen as "universal." Although these ideas will differ from context to context, everyone has a culture and *almost* everyone has faith, religious belief, or spiritual aspects to their life. Hence, the designation of humanitarian needs as universal is ultimately a secular interpretation of what is universal. A person does not necessarily become void of their cultural and religious identity because they have experienced a disaster. In fact, faith was one of the central elements of individual, family, and community response to Typhoon Haiyan, as indicated in conversations with affected people.

As a means to overcome some of the barriers, NGO respondents generally were against religious literacy training per se, but very much in favour of alternatives to training, including debriefings or informal forums at which people could exchange knowledge and ask questions that might seem "stupid," as one NGO respondent put it. For instance, a national staff member said that no one had asked them "when do you go to church?", and so they had not gone at all even though they wanted to, especially in the emergency phase when it would have been personally beneficial. Consequently, structural secularity compromised individual well-being. The "one-stop shop trainings" were criticised for not allowing these types of discussion spaces.

Furthermore, the analysis of secularity in the humanitarian response to Haiyan should not be taken as an indictment of the secular approach in humanitarian response. As Mahmood (2016) put it, "[a] scholarly inquiry into secularism's promise, limits, and contradictions should not be mistaken as a denunciation of secularism or as a call for its demise." It must be remembered that many NGO staff members thought that secularity allowed for a space in which many cultures could work together in the response, meaning that a focus on vital needs was ensured, and that they would enjoy increased access to people. Disaster-affected people I spoke with also appreciated and held in high esteem the work of some secular organisations.

Similar problems were faced by secular and faith-based organisations, such as power imbalances vis-à-vis beneficiary selection. International faith-based organisations do not necessarily know better, as they struggle too with cultural dissonance between countries, as recounted by De Cordier (2009) in relation to Western-based Muslim aid organisations working in Muslim countries in other regions, and by Palmer (2011) specifically with regard to Islamic Relief Worldwide and Rohingya refugees from Myanmar in Bangladesh. A common faith affiliation is not necessarily sufficient to bridge cultural divides. Many underlying commonalities between different types of organisation also show that secular or religious lacunae are not the most divisive of problems, while remaining a worthwhile lens for analysis.

Following on from Asad's dismissal of the neutrality of secularism, the secularism of the Filipino governance system had not guaranteed tolerance and equality but allowed for "different structures of ambition and fear," (Asad 2003, p. 8) of which the people were well aware and highly critical. This was highly damaging in the Filipino context for the NGO's perceived impartiality, neutrality, and transparency in the eyes of the affected population, with some secular organisations even being reportedly banned from communities for being too politically involved. Likewise, as pointed out by a respondent, definitions of secularity are different in different contexts and the secularism of the Filipino government officials was still highly linked to religious beliefs, with the government still influenced by pressure from religious leaders. Secular staff reported that they felt "awkward" with the amount of religion evidenced in interactions with government officials. This shows a difference in the extent to which religion is privatised in differing conceptions of secularity, meaning that expectations of where secular boundaries fell were different between secular Filipino organisations and secular European organisations. Equally this shows the socially constructed nature of the secular as appropriate to different cultures and countries. One example is the restrictions around reproductive health that are followed by the government but seen as highly religious by internationals. This was most concretely demonstrated in partnership of secular INGOs with secular local partners who would then partner with faith-based local organisations. By adding an extra step of removal, a process of boundary-moving could occur, leaving the secular INGOs satisfied with the local secular partner and the local secular partner able to utilise funds for local FBOs that might otherwise not have been acceptable. In this way, local secular organisations can act as a form of cultural broker (Browne 2015, p. 23), able to navigate between differing secularisms to understand both what is expected internationally and what is normal locally.

Yet, it seems that in privatising religion and culture, and emphasising the material, technological, and the bureaucratic, secular humanitarian organisations have lost an element of the social and the personal in their interactions. This was the effect of functional secularism across the humanitarian system, impacting on any organisation, secular or faith-based, that tried to fit into the secular norms of this system. The findings of this research encourage a shift in emphasis from outcomes of humanitarian action to the process and methods of the action. Also, key is how delivery methods can be improved to enhance interaction with beneficiaries rather than prioritising only the timeliness of distributions. Interestingly, smaller, local faith-based organisations, criticised by some NGO staff members for not being fully coordinated with the humanitarian system, have reaped one advantage in their disassociation, remaining more in touch, in many cases, with people in affected areas and thus becoming more highly regarded.

Conclusion

The dominant secular culture was maintained in the response. Respondents from FBOs said they felt the influence of a dominant secular culture in the way local organisations, particularly those that were faith-based were treated in the international response. As one respondent said, "the local church knowledge has been overlooked." Likewise, international staff noted that in the emergency differences between organisations based on secular or faith-based values are not clear, especially as all are coordinated through the cluster system. In this way the cluster system acts as the leveller as all organisations are brought within the standards of the secularised system. As one international staff member for an FBO put it, "through this coordination, the community perceives them [the secular and faith-based organisations] as the same." Functional secularism in the humanitarian system created a system of boundary-making and led to a lack of clarity about boundary-breaking. When put to people who had experienced a humanitarian response, it became clear that the biggest obstacle to overcome concerned personal and human interaction. Efforts were made in the Haiyan response to enhance accountability and contact with affected people, but the study's findings demonstrate that this move in humanitarianism is still nascent and has yet to affect the overall status quo of the humanitarian system. While the accountability agenda speaks to elements broader than secular and religious tensions, the spotlight on the effects of functional secularism in the humanitarian system has illuminated perceived and appreciated differences between types of organisations. This has helped to increase the focus on the importance and the centrality of improving human interaction between organisations and beneficiaries in humanitarian response. Through careful coding of qualitative data, factors emerged that were commonly used to describe a secular approach to humanitarian response. Secularity was employed as a boundary-making tool in the response to Typhoon Haiyan. One of the standout quotations in this regard was "faith can come in, but not religion." Secular humanitarianism was shown to be flexible and receptive enough to people's personal faith, such as prayer, but there was a line of demarcation: anything more, such as the repairing of churches, was deemed to be inappropriate. The implications for the humanitarian system centre on the unknown and *ad hoc* nature of decisions about when boundaries can be broken. Those of managerial staff were not necessarily well informed and more could be done to capture local field staff knowledge to ensure local cultural relevance. For localisation and accountability agendas to be realised, international humanitarian actors must contend with their own biases. The research implications underline that secular values prioritising technical foci alone undermine accountability to affected populations owing to a lack of human interaction. In addition, secular values treating religious institutions and communities with suspicion limit opportunities for local partnerships.

Bibliography

Ager, A., and Ager, J., 2015. *Faith, Secularism, and Humanitarian Engagement: Finding the Place of Religion in the Support of Displaced Communities*. New York: Palgrave Macmillan.

ALNAP, 2006. *Evaluating Humanitarian Action Using the OECD-DAC Criteria: An ALNAP Guide for Humanitarian Agencies.* London: Overseas Development Institute.

Asad, T., 2003. *Formations of the Secular: Christianity, Islam, Modernity.* Stanford, CA: Stanford University Press.

Bailey, S., and Pavanello, S., 2009. *Untangling Early Recovery.* London: Overseas Development Institute, Humanitarian Policy Group, No. 38.

Browne, K.E., 2015. *Standing in the Need: Culture, Comfort, and Coming Home After Katrina.* Austin: University of Texas Press.

Buckley, D., 2017. *Faithful to Secularism: The Religious Politics of Democracy in Ireland, Senegal, and the Philippines.* 1st ed. New York City: Columbia University Press.

Corpus, O.J., Flores, J.M., and Combinido, P., 2015. *Obliged to be Grateful: How Local Communities Experienced Humanitarian Actors in the Haiyan Response.* Woking: Plan International.

De Cordier, B., 2009. Faith-Based Aid, Globalisation and the Humanitarian Frontline. An Operational Analysis of Western-Based Muslim Aid Organisations. *Disasters,* 33 (4), 608–628.

Fiddian-Qasmiyeh, E., 2011. The Pragmatics of Performance: Putting 'Faith' in Aid in the Sahrawi Refugee Camps. *Journal of Refugee Studies,* 24 (3), 533–547.

Hanley, T., Binas, R., Murray, J., and Tribunalo, B., 2014. *IASC Inter-agency Humanitarian Evaluation of the Typhoon Haiyan Response.* New York: UNOCHA, Inter-Agency Humanitarian Evaluation Steering Group.

Lau, A.L., and Cornelio, J.S., 2015. Tzu Chi and the Philanthropy of Filipino Volunteers. *Asian Journal of Social Science,* 43 (4), 376–399.

Mahmood, S., 2016. Religious Difference in a Secular Age: A Minority Report—An Introduction. *The Immanent Frame* (blog). http://blogs.ssrc.org/tif/2016/02/09/religious-difference-in-a-secular-age-a-minority-report-an-introduction/.

Ong, J.C., Flores, J.M., and Combinido, P., 2015. Obliged to Be Grateful: How Local Communities Experienced Humanitarian Actors in the Haiyan Response. Woking: Plan International.

Palmer, V., 2011. Analysing Cultural Proximity: Islamic Relief Worldwide and Rohingya Refugees in Bangladesh. *Development in Practice,* 21 (1), 96–108.

Taylor, C., 2007. *A Secular Age.* Harvard: Harvard University Press.

Thaut, L.C., 2009. The Role of Faith in Christian Faith-Based Humanitarian Agencies: Constructing the Taxonomy. *Voluntas,* 20 (4), 319–50.

Wilkinson, O., 2014. "Is There a Secular Humanitarian Faith?" *The Religion Factor* (blog). https://www.rug.nl/research/centre-for-religious-studies/religion-conflict-globalization/blog/is-there-a-secular-humanitarian-faith-24-09-2014.

Yacat, J., 2013. Filipino Psychology (Sikolohiyang Pilipino). *In:* K.D. Keith, ed. *The Encyclopedia of Cross-Cultural Psychology.* Hoboken, NJ: Wiley-Blackwell.

5 Evolving secular-religious dynamics in the humanitarian system

The humanitarian system's current trends show the continued relevance of secular-religious dynamics. Looking at the World Humanitarian Summit and the following trend of localisation, as well as using further findings from the Typhoon Haiyan response, the first part of this chapter unpacks how secularity underlines tensions in localisation and highlights why a different way forward is needed. Thinking of next steps, the second part of this chapter suggests that there is a need for post-secular reflexivity and religious literacy in the humanitarian system to help counter some of the negative effects of secular-religious dynamics.

Current humanitarian trends and difficulties in secular-religious dynamics

This section presents evidence from two angles: first, from the practical aspects of the humanitarian response to Typhoon Haiyan and, second, from the global policy process and international norms shifts around the World Humanitarian Summit and localisation. From both cases, we see that difficulties with secular and religious dynamics are ingrained into the processes. Scholars have warned against the ways in which these secular-religious stereotypes can settle in our minds and affect international systems. Even when religious engagement happens, we are stuck in a repeating cycle of framing religious beliefs and practices as either "good" or "bad" (Hurd 2015), which only has the potential to worsen as "the persistence and even vigorous resurgence of religious forms that are often conservative with regard to women's rights present threats to hard-won gender achievements over recent decades" (Tomalin 2015, p. 65), as Tomalin notes in regards to women's rights but with relevance to all rights that are significant for humanitarian response. As the perceived threats rise, secular humanitarians could see an increase in anxieties around religious influence and embed itself in destructive good/bad binaries.

"Bad" religion stereotypes are pervasive and very much linked to real world examples, such as reports of moral corruption and partiality among some FBOs (Flanigan 2009), or the influence of American Evangelical NGOs, in one example from Fiddian-Qasmiyeh (2015), as powerfully advocating for some crisis affected people but marginalising others. It is worth reiterating the underlying assertion that secular and religious dynamics are never neutral and the forces of faith in FBOs can have conflicting positive and negative effects. Nevertheless, secular boundary-making has brought secular actors to a point of misidentification of the problems with FBOs. Fountain points out in Flanigan's critique of FBOs that,

> The author's case rests upon a simplistic associative logic (evangelism = oppression) deeply ingrained in the genealogy of development as 'secular' moral goodness which traces its roots back to a rejection of Christian mission; a rejection which still inheres in the concept of development today and haunts ongoing attempts, including Flanigan's, to separate 'good' development from religious taintings.
>
> (Fountain 2011, p. 156)

Various authors have made a sustained attempt to re-frame the "evangelism = oppression" narrative for humanitarianism (while still very much affirming that coercive proselytisation is morally wrong) and the broader good/ bad religion framing for international relations (Hurd 2015, pp. 25–26). Fiddian-Qasmiyeh highlights the agency of so-called beneficiaries to ignore proselytisation and even use it to their advantage (Fiddian-Qasmiyeh 2011). Mahmood famously broke open conceptions of conservative religion with her monograph on the ways in which women are involved in and support the women's mosque movement as part of the Islamist Revival in Cairo, Egypt (Mahmood 2011). Tomalin echoes that there is concern that secularism is bad for women as we then ignore the ways in which privatising religion has made religious beliefs and practices confined to domestic spaces alone for women (Tomalin 2015, p. 73). Lynch and Schwarz (2017, p. 642) highlight the various types of secular proselytism at play in humanitarian response, namely "donor proselytism" that assumes "the giver knows best" and leads to the operationalisation of neoliberal governmentality through requirements from donors.

There is a continued assumption that old-fashioned secularity that privatises and marginalises will be sufficient to keep the "bad" religion away, without critical self-reflection about the other influencing factors that feed into the creation of "bad" religion and the reality that

> theories of secularisation and the ideology of secularism simply no longer seem to fit the evidence or function persuasively in many

contexts, and as such could be viewed as outmoded and even Eurocentric tools for dealing with the serious issues of women's [and men's] global disadvantage.

(Tomalin 2015, p. 65)

Alongside this, the reality of neoliberal pressures on humanitarian response to create "resilient" subjects has led to a dangerous position in which there is "a marked difference between the autonomy of the resourceful as opposed to the interventionist strategies of resilience" (Evans and Reid 2014, p. 90). FBOs *and* secular organisations can be affected by this neoliberal governmentality (Atalay 2019).

The secularity that is tied to neoliberalism undercuts the autonomy and agency of disaster-affected people of diverse and no faiths. As Mahmood carefully explains, secularity offers protections, but it has created its own systems of repression. Mahmood speaks of political secularism, but it is also relevant to secularity in the humanitarian system. She says that secularism offers the protection of

individuals and religious minorities to hold and practice their religious beliefs freely without state or social coercion . . . its guarantee that a citizen's religious affiliation is inconsequential to her civil and political status in the eyes of the law . . . that it allows believers and nonbelievers to speak their mind without fear of state or social discrimination.

(Mahmood 2015, p. 20)

For humanitarianism, this translates to the principles of impartiality and neutrality – that religious beliefs and practice will not deny anyone humanitarian assistance if they are in need. Yet with the backdrop of these protections still in mind, Mahmood affirms that secularism

also entails the reordering and remaking of religious life and interconfessional relations in accord with specific norms, themselves foreign to the life of the religions and peoples it organises. This dimension of political secularism – shot through as it is with paradoxes and instabilities – needs to be understood for the life worlds it creates, the forms of exclusion and violence it entails, the kinds of hierarchies it generates, and those it seeks to undermine.

(Mahmood 2015, p. 21)

In relation to secular humanitarianism, we see the lauding of the protections, but we do not have sufficient analysis of the way in which an influx of external humanitarian organisations can form a microcosm of a secular public sphere in an emergency that thinks it allows for the protections listed first previously, which in some ways it achieves, but is unaware of the exclusions, hierarchies, and occasional violence it produces as well. Turning to the two cases, I will look specifically at the failures and disjunctures, before offering some ways forward in the final section.

Typhoon Haiyan response

After Typhoon Haiyan, humanitarian staff had faced many challenges related to secular-religious dynamics that they navigated with differing degrees of success. One challenge was that they did not know how to engage with religious groups without fear that other groups would feel marginalised. A national staff member of a secular organisation noted there were communities with five or so main faith groups and said faith can be divisive in these communities at times. An international staff member added that denominational differences could cause splits in the community. Although instances of churches exclusively giving to their congregations were recounted second hand (no interviewee had directly encountered this), these stories also provided fuel for fearfulness about how to engage religious groups without biasing humanitarian assistance. One international staff member for an FBO recounted an example of having to explain to religious partners that beneficiaries were not required to attend religious ceremonies to receive aid. There had been considerable negotiation. The compromise in this case was that ceremonies could proceed but it had to be voluntary for beneficiaries to attend. Another example from a national staff member related to the importance of blessings. It was reported that people did not want to resettle in certain areas because of bad spirits, and even though it took a bit more time, it was necessary for the area to be blessed so that shelter projects could move ahead.

Another area of difficulty was partnerships with local faith actors. It has long been advocated that INGOs partner with local organisations to both deliver their programming and build up the capacity of the local organisations at the same time (Eade 1997). The advantages to working with local partners are well documented. A coalition of organisations (Christian Aid, CAFOD, Oxfam, Tearfund, ActionAid) came together to review the response to Haiyan from the perspective of partnerships with local organisations. The findings of this study highlighted several ways in which partnerships are highly advantageous. First, national NGOs' knowledge of local culture and politics was invaluable in many instances. It was through knowledge of local politics that they could act impartially, not their outsider status. In fact, it was the INGOs that too quickly aligned themselves with the Local Government Units (LGUs) to the dissatisfaction of the local NGOs (Featherstone 2014, p. 9). This local knowledge both means greater relevance and appropriateness of programming and facilitates communication and understanding between INGOs and the communities they aim to serve (Featherstone 2014, p. 4). FBOs were particularly highlighted as those that work closely with communities, thanks in part to their widespread networks in communities that allowed them to have "a far greater depth of reach than many INGOs" (Featherstone 2014, p. 9). FBOs were highlighted for their ability to both maintain a local base but quickly draw on international funding to respond to the disaster. Finally, with information from another evaluation, local organisations, again with FBOs particularly in mind, were able to quickly mobilise volunteers to aid the response, who were also able to reach more remote destinations (Sanderson and Delica Willison 2014, p. 7).

However, the reality of partnering with local organisations can often be fraught with difficulties. One of the main problems was the impenetrability of the cluster system populated by the large INGOs. As Featherstone (2014, p. 20) sums up,

> Staff capacity limitations, a lack of familiarity with the international humanitarian architecture, poor access to transport, the long distance between field sites and coordination hubs exacerbated by the predilection for having meetings at the end of the day (making it impossible to return on public transport) were all obstacles to NNGO participation in Clusters.

One interviewee told Tamminga and Redheffer (2014, p. 9) that "Clusters are an exclusive club. Local organisations aren't participating because they aren't accessible. It's hard to find out where they're meeting," as has been noted in other evaluations (Hanley *et al.* 2014). Parallel coordination mechanisms exist meaning that the INGOs organised themselves through the cluster system, while other actors used their own forums to organise response. This was echoed in my discussions with people following Haiyan relating to secular-religious dynamics. People from the Philippines could often feel pushed out of the conversation especially in cluster meetings. As one staff member for a nationally focused FBO recounted, it was a task to process how to be a person of faith pulled into a disaster response. They said,

> It was interesting to be someone who spent time at the grassroots and then get pulled into a cluster meeting. They have high-powered cluster meetings, and they are looking at maps in places where we've been working for years. Some stuff was uncomfortable. I would show up with two [religious leaders] that were well connected in the island, but

the expats were making the decisions. The people who were Filipino in the field were pushed to the side.

The staff member did not feel there was a stereotyping of the religious leaders however, but that the divide was about power and prestige in the international system. They said, "Your logo dictated where you fell in the room." The higher logos were of the international NGOs, mostly secular, and not local. Another national staff member with experience internationally said that they were taken aback when attending cluster meetings in the Philippines and realised "Am I like this in other countries?" They described the experience as a "wake up call" for their work in other countries.

There was a particular gap in partnership with some local faith actors. A national staff member for a secular organisation explained that their organisation was the first to contact a church that had been serving affected people for four months already. They explained that the church leaders had tried to attend the clusters at the beginning of the response "but the organisations don't think about [the local faith actors] in the longer term for partnerships." There needs to be capacity built for disaster response with all Civil Society Organisations (CSOs), including local faith actors. Again, international FBOs noted that a lot of these church partners do not have sufficient capacity to work with them, but then secular organisations also have these problems with other CSOs. FBOs were more likely to partner with local faith actors and other FBOs. Within FBOs there was a divide between Catholic and Protestant denominations, where each worked within their own denomination for the most part. An interviewee pointed out that local CSOs play a bridging role for secular and religious tensions around funding and donor requirements. CSOs work closely with religious institutions while remaining broadly secular themselves. It is therefore acceptable for an international secular NGO to fund these CSOs who can then fund services that through religious institutions. This is differentiation and offsetting as a secular move to distance from religious influence, while still using its influence and advantages. One advantage of religious resources, however, is that unrestricted funding from private religious individuals and groups can allow freedom not given by strict time frames from the large institutional donors and act as a relatively secure source of funds in comparison to the whims of donor governments and other private donations that are affected by economic markets and recessions (Hopgood and Vinjamuri 2012).

Many of these points have been reiterated in analyses of other responses and the work of humanitarian actors in general (Ramalingam *et al.* 2013; Charter 4 Change 2015; Tanner and Moro 2016; Wall and Hedlund 2016; de Geoffroy *et al.* 2017; Wilkinson and Ager 2017; Wilkinson 2018a; CARE *et al.* 2019). The same issues of little direct funding to NNGOs, weaknesses in partnerships and lack of decision-making power for local actors, and the burden of donor requirements/lack of capacity to meet donor requirements often arise. The added element from a secular-religious analysis demonstrates that divisions can be based on suspicions – and realities – of "bad" religion, such as conflicts among denominations and aid tied to religious ceremonies, which then drives a distancing from all local faith actors, even when they could be key local partners.

World humanitarian summit and localisation

The Grand Bargain (Inter-Agency Standing Committee 2018) process as part of the World Humanitarian Summit, affirmed nine key areas of action. The second of these particularly focuses on the issue of localisation, or the recognition that humanitarian response should be "as local as possible, as international as necessary" (UNSG 2016b). As reported in 2019, signatories to the Grand Bargain are particularly committed to localisation in comparison to some of the other areas and 81% feel that they are making good progress in this area (Metcalfe-Hough *et al.* 2019, p. 34). Progress remains unclear on reaching 25% of funding directly to NNGOs, but it seems that there has only been

> a slight increase in direct funding to national and local NGOs, from 1.7% of all NGO funding in 2016 to 2.7% in 2017. But local and national NGOs received just 0.4% directly of all international humanitarian assistance reported to FTS in 2017, a rise of just 0.1% from 2016.
>
> (Urquhart and Tuchel 2018, p. 11)

There is no data to indicate secular or faith-based distinctions in this regard, but some of these local actors will be local faith actors as it is clear that many local actors are also faith-based. In an earlier survey, UNFPA found that 85% of their country offices worked with faith actors, but 10% of those stated that they like to keep this "out of the official limelight" (Karam 2018, p. 135) due to various fears. Likewise, as Karam points out,

> many FBOs, while serving large segments of the local populations at the most micro-community levels, have no interest in or resources for a presence at Western headquarters. . . . And yet they are critical development actors. In some ways FBO engagement with the global development agenda has been, arguably, almost class based. The "elite" FBOs are the ones at the table.
>
> (Karam 2018, p. 139)

Any secular organisation that just works with elite FBOs, and not the local faith actors, therefore, is not seeing the full picture. Furthermore, the elite FBOs have a duty to bring these local modalities to the fore in international fora. The elite FBOs also only represent a certain segment of the full range of international, national, and local FBOs. As Deneulin points out, "the development community is often seen to be biased in favour of so-called 'progressive' forces within a religious tradition who share common points with those holding a secular worldview" (Deneulin and Bano 2009, p. 25). The nuances of partnering with local faith actors should, therefore, be part of localisation.

The World Humanitarian Summit, at which the Grand Bargain was presented, was an interesting exercise in secular boundary-making itself. I was fortunate to attend in May 2016. The Summit was organised in terms of political hierarchies, with the highest-level leaders attending 7 key roundtables, 15 invitation-only special sessions made up of governmental, intergovernmental, and NGO representatives, and then over 100 side events. While none of the roundtables had a specific focus on religion, 2 of the 15 special sessions focused on elements of religion, with one on "Religious Engagement: The Contributions of Faith Communities to our Shared Humanity" and the other on "Islamic Social Financing." Only one of the side events had a specifically religious focus, which was the Joint Learning Initiative on Faith & Local Communities (JLI) and Soka Gakkai International (SGI)'s "One Humanity, Shared Responsibilities: Evidence for Religious Groups' Contributions to Humanitarian Response" event. It is likely that the role of religion will have some up in some of the other events, however, as there were discussions about increasing participation of beneficiaries and working with local actors. There had been considerable efforts by the JLI and its members to ensure that the question of religious engagement was part of the higher-level discussions, and the inclusion in the special sessions could be seen as a moment of secular-religious rapprochement. Yet it is also noticeable that the attention towards Islamic social financing had an instrumentalist twinge, as secular humanitarians gathered round to find out if they could diversify their funding sources from this stream of financing. Likewise, in the months before the Summit, there was a convening in New York, not very subtly titled "Religious Resourcing for Humanitarian Efforts" (UN Inter-Agency Task Force for Engaging with Faith-Based Organisations 2016). At this event the "elite" FBOs were able to speak to the UN system about the difficulties with resourcing, including increased restrictions on Muslim organisations, and the need to think about multi-year financing to join humanitarian-development-peace efforts in which FBOs are involved. Although the FBOs were able to push back somewhat, the overall effect was an instrumentalising interest in religious resources (human, social, and financial).

It is the after-effects of the Summit, however, that particularly demonstrate the secular boundary-making that occurred. While it would not be expected that secular-religious engagement became a particular commitment from the Summit among the plethora of other issues at hand, it was notable that no mention of faith-based activity or secular-religious engagement was made in the Chair's Summary (UNSG 2016a). In the Commitments to Action summary report (World Humanitarian Summit 2016b), it was noted that 160 FBOs signed the Charter for Faith-Based Humanitarian Action (World Humanitarian Summit 2016a), but this was the only reference and very much kept faith-based humanitarian action in its corner. In the Report of the Secretary General to the UN's General Assembly on the Summit (UNSG 2016c), the language notably makes requirements of FBOs, stating that they will "use their networks to raise awareness for compliance with international humanitarian law and humanitarian principles" (para 20) and

> Civil society, such as international and local non-governmental organisations, as well as faith-based groups, diaspora and migrant communities and others, must continue to fulfil their critical role in providing leadership, service delivery, advocacy and outreach, including through engagement with affected communities.

(para 82)

To paraphrase and translate through a secular humanitarian lens, FBOs should make sure other FBOs abide by the humanitarian principles, because this is one of the areas where the humanitarian system judges faith influence to be a problem. Furthermore, as part of civil society that is well connected to the local community, FBOs should continue in the role they already play and the international humanitarian systems is comfortable with, i.e., helping the system to connect to local communities. The secular boundary-making process that was revealed to have happened throughout was to allow FBOs a place at the table to some extent, but then to marginalise and instrumentalise the commitments that the FBOs made, keeping them separate from the main fray, but asking for changes and support when and where the humanitarian system wants and needs it. There was a decided lack of mutuality.

Likewise, in the UN Inter-Agency Task Force on Religion and Development, the elite FBOs, with some of the more national FBOs that see worth in an international presence at UN Headquarters (HQ), gather to discuss within their own circles. Having attended several of these meetings, I mean this as no insult to the organisers who work tirelessly within the confines of the strict political structure of the UN to find space and legitimacy for such gatherings. Nevertheless, it remains the case that it is the faith-based actors and those interested in religion and development research and practice, such as myself, that attend these events. Azza Karam, the lead of the Task Force, notes that recent years have seen several advancements in the role of FBOs, but that the rise in secular interest has taken a transactional value and thus risks repeating many of the errors (with neo-colonial, instrumentalising connotations) of the past (Karam 2019). The fact that secularity has engaged with religion only through a wish to counter violent extremism, put restrictions on some, and cherry pick progressive others, highlights "the limited effectiveness of current attempts at engaging with religion" (Deneulin and Bano 2009, p. 25). I hasten to add that this is only about development, not the humanitarian system, which the evidence has shown is potentially even more ingrained in secular positions and sees religion and culture as the messy stuff that development actors should deal with. The next step in convening is, ultimately, to stop elite FBOs reporting back to each other and start communicating more strategically outwards, encouraging post-secular reflexivity and religious literacy, as will be discussed in this next section.

Bridging boundaries: what to do next?

It is tempting to give some remedy and have some final recommendations that will ultimately soften some of the criticisms of the secular-religious dynamics that have been at play in the examples in this chapter and previous chapters. There is no silver bullet but it is possible to pinpoint the practical difficulties that need solutions from the Typhoon Haiyan response (people knew the problems, just not what to do about it) and global policy processes, such as the World Humanitarian Summit (people are interested in religious engagement, but do not know how to do it in non-instrumental and stereotyping, "good/bad" religion ways) and help move towards a reframing of secular-religious dynamics that could help the humanitarian system in the future.

The first aspect is to look towards sociological theory for tips on how to reconsider secular positioning. Berger, once famous for secularisation, has moved towards pluralism as his response (Berger 2014). This is more than religious tolerance alone, as tolerance is created through the maintenance of the public/private divide (Wilson 2012, p. 111) and therefore a further manifestation of secularism. We must push beyond toleration, to reflection and engagement. Alongside pluralism and globalisation, post-secularism has been a relatively recent trend. Scholars have asked if a "post-secular rapprochement" is possible (Cloke and Beaumont 2013; Cloke 2011) and asserted how the post-secular is useful in bridging secular-religious divides in international relations (Mavelli and Petito 2014a). The danger of course is that the "post-secular" is just yet another manifestation of Judeo-Christian

European secular hegemony (Mahmood 2015, p. 8), yet several authors are building the ways in which it is relevant to the international political sphere (Wilson 2014; Mavelli and Petito 2014b; Wilkinson 2018b), of which the humanitarian system is a part, not least because this sphere replicates European particularity. Of note, the prefix "post-" would suggest that the concept is situated chronologically after secularisation, which in turn suggests that secularisation has stopped and the concept is no longer relevant. This is an overly reductive position that disregards the wealth of debate around the post-secular. The position adopted herein instead proposes that the secular and post-secular can exist concurrently and that the post-secular builds on the secular.

Ager and Ager (2011) placed humanitarian action within a post-secular world for the first time with reference to Habermas. Merli (2012, p. 48) similarly noted the use of Habermasian post-secularism for research on religion and disaster not soon after. Habermas sees a religious resurgence in the modern, globalised world that has encouraged a "change in consciousness" (Habermas 2008, p. 20) in Europe. Three phenomena are noted as offering evidence of this change in consciousness: 1) where once secularisation seemed to be the goal that the world would work towards, the secular person can no longer assume that modernisation will necessarily lead to secularisation. Secular Europeans are made aware of their relativity in the global environment, 2) religion exists firmly in the public sphere as well as the private. Religious organisations and institutions "can attain influence on public opinion and will formation by making relevant contributions to key issues, irrespective of whether their arguments are convincing or objectionable" (Habermas 2008, p. 20); p. 3) Migration and reception of refugees have introduced forms of traditional culture into European life. This leads Habermas to reflect on the problems of multiculturalism, pluralism, and secularism in which equality is expected for all, but different proponents would understand that equality in different ways. The question is whether integration and equality mean the full recognition of all forms of religious life and practice or whether participation in the public sphere necessitates a separation from religion. He claims that we all too often live in an "uneasy modus vivendi" (Habermas 2008, p. 22) in which a form of mere tolerance is practiced rather than full openness to all. He thus suggests that a process of "complementary learning" is preferable. This asks that secular people, rather than assuming their dominance in the secular public sphere, also put effort into how they interact with religious voices and beliefs in the public spheres, just as religious people must "translate" their beliefs in secular discourse for it to be understandable in the public sphere. This demands a reappraisal from secular people of how they interact with religion in society. The secular mindset is not simply a default position without reflexivity, but a choice in which the secular thinker should comprehend the weight of their own position.

This is the continued dialogue between the religious and secular mindset that characterises the post-secular public sphere in which differing interpretations of life are admitted. The main growth of the international humanitarian system has only occurred in the last 25 years (Barnett and Weiss 2011, p. 27), at the same time that a global "resurgence of religion" has been noted. Tracking this resurgence, the contemporary structure of the secular humanitarian system has struggled and will continue to struggle with the important role but also changing face of religion in crises worldwide. It is proposed that the humanitarian system has maintained a course of "mere tolerance" in the first part of the new millennium in line with a "Westphalian presumption," "that religious and cultural pluralism cannot be accommodated in international society, but must be privatised, marginalised, or even overcome – by an ethic of cosmopolitanism – if there is to be international order" (Thomas 2000, p. 815). Yet in order to proceed effectively, secular humanitarians must promote a process of "complementary learning," as suggested by Habermas. The position of a secular person is not without its demands. The secular person has a burden to understand the religious, just as the religious should try to understand the secular. As Habermas puts it, "the West is one participant among others, and all participants must be willing to be enlightened by others about their respective blind spots" (Mendieta 2010). The humanitarian system has secular blind spots and there is, therefore, space for eye-opening reflection.

This does not mean that the secular humanitarian must bend to accept truth claims from religious belief. As Habermas explains it is perfectly possible for this person to remain "agnostic" (Habermas 2006, pp. 16–17), while highly engaged in this complementary learning. As Junker-Kenny explains, "the crucial difference for Habermas is between 'learning processes,' which should be open to consider other truth claims, and 'outcome,' which should not be religiously biased in order to be 'acceptable not just for the members of one religious community'" (Junker-Kenny 2011, p. 141). There is certainly no implication that the post-secular asks secular humanitarians to follow others' religious practices or beliefs, but it asks for a halt to marginalisation and privatisation of religion in humanitarian learning processes. This may be the point at which Habermasian post-secularism does not go far enough for some as there is a derogation of religious thought in the ultimate outcome, but in line with a type of pluralism encountered in humanitarian settings, both internal to organisations and in conversation with crisis-affected communities, this is a practical means for allowing learning processes between all, while also allowing for a path of moderation to open up.

There are many critiques of Habermasian post-secularism (for example, Dillon 2010; Beckford 2012), mostly pinpointing that he does not go far enough in encouraging rapprochement and maintains a secular outlook on the post-secular, but I have argued elsewhere (Wilkinson 2018b) that this is precisely why Habermasian post-secularism is useful for the humanitarian system. First, many of the norms created in the international humanitarian system emanate from a hegemonic European secularist worldview, coming from Brussels and Geneva and reflecting internal tensions, scepticism, anxiety, and dismissal of religion in those settings. Second, if secular humanitarians are to conceive of religious belief and practice in the humanitarian system, then Habermas' secular take on post-secularism seems like the best place to start. It is precisely because it does not push for more that Habermasian post-secularism is a convincing, challenging, but not too threatening, angle. It is worth underlining that Habermas "can be read as a sustained attempt . . . to elaborate the human orientation towards cooperation" (Junker-Kenny 2011, p. 2) rather than individualism. He has spent his life's work considering the ways in which we communicate with each other for consensus. Junker-Kenny underlines that Habermas does not merely seek to instrumentalise religious belief "for the functional reasons of motivating or stabilising democratic society, but for reasons of a content only religion can provide" (Junker-Kenny 2011, p. 135). Against the criticisms, Habermas demonstrates his own post-secular reflexivity to learn from and truly engage with religious content for its inherent worth. Habermasian post-secularism does not provide a set of clearly defined instructions for changes in the humanitarian system yet it is an approachable theory for secular humanitarians and therefore potentially more persuasive.

For secular humanitarians, the key learning is secular reflexivity. The post-secular approach encourages those operating in an overall secular paradigm to self-reflexively consider their own methods of communication in order to improve their interaction with those not in the same paradigm. As Habermas asserts,

> secular citizens are likewise not spared a cognitive burden, because a secularist attitude does not suffice for the expected cooperation with fellow citizens who are religious. This cognitive act of adaptation needs to be distinguished from the political virtue of mere tolerance.
>
> (Habermas 2006, p. 15)

On the one hand, in a critical appraisal of the principle of impartiality it becomes little more than "mere tolerance": the act of non-discrimination through the tolerance of all, but the comprehension of few. On the other hand, in a more positive light, the humanitarian principles could in fact allow the space in which the post-secular can flourish by allowing for interaction that may not have happened without neutrality and impartiality through access, communication, and cooperation between different people and organisations. This refreshed conceptualisation of the humanitarian principles puts the emphasis on post-secular reflexivity to open up secular humanitarians to new worlds of thought and practice, while coupled with religious literacy to engage thoughtfully and consciously with secular-religious dynamics in humanitarian response.

Religious literacy constitutes the thought process through which newly reflexive, post-secular humanitarians can start to rethink their approach to religious belief and practice. There is evidence that practitioners want to have more nuanced understanding in this regard (Bush, Fountain, and Feener 2015, p. 8). The Harvard Religious Literacy project describes religious literacy in four key aspects. First, that there must be a differentiation between devotional expression and the study of religion, that is to say that the study of religion recognises "the validity of normative theological assertions without equating them with universal truths about the tradition itself" (Moore 2015, p. 1). One group's assertions are valid as normative for them, but they are not equated with the whole tradition. An example of a common mistake, therefore, is to think that Muslim women are oppressed and equate that as an identifier of the whole religion when in fact there are a plethora of internal debates and representations of the role of women in Islam. The three other principles are summed up as:

1. religions are internally diverse as opposed to uniform; 2. religions evolve and change over time as opposed to being ahistorical and static; 3. religious influences are embedded in all dimensions of culture as opposed to the assumption that religions function in discrete, isolated, "private" contexts.

(Moore 2015, p. 2)

Bush, Fountain, and Feener explain that religious literacy for them "includes familiarity with debates about the contested meanings of 'religion' and critical attention to concepts and practices of the 'secular'" (Bush *et al.* 2015, p. 4). Religious literacy does not require an incredibly detailed knowledge of the main tenets of different religions, but it is instead the "critical capacity for locating the discourses and practices of religion within their specific social and political contexts" (Bush *et al.* 2015, p. 4). For them, the post-secular reflexive turn for secular humanitarians is already built into this concept of religious as a key part of the process. Tomalin describes religious literacy as

enhancing knowledge of the importance of religions in people's lives in both developing and developed societies; learning about the beliefs and practices embodied within different religious traditions; and moving beyond Western ways of viewing the nature and role of religion largely informed by Christian experiences.

(Tomalin 2015, pp. 68–69)

She argues that the third element of this has been particularly overlooked, hence the need for a nuanced engagement with what this might look like and include, which is why I affirm the need for such a book as this that looks at the question of the secular as much as the religious and thinks through what a post-secular rapprochement might include.

Speaking with humanitarians in the Philippines, most had some levels of awareness of these points, but they were very vague and based on instinct rather than anything more thorough. To demonstrate a few examples of this awareness, one international staff member for a secular organisation explained that people do try to take these things into account, but the generic frameworks that do not include the local context they use for implementation can be a vacuum, creating challenges about how to engage. This leaves organisations open to seeming two-faced when they say they are participatory but then make decisions that are contrary to the local culture, as this staff member explained. Another international staff member said that this means organisations often ignore these more "awkward" issues, as they put it. In another way, the problem was even subtler. As one international staff member explained, just because people say they are Catholic, it does not mean they have a strong faith. Likewise, another international staff member said that there are those who are more secular in their Catholicism and then others, especially in rural areas, who bring indigenous beliefs and practices into their Christianity, to make the religion very different to Christianity experienced in other countries, such as European countries. There can be a danger in putting too much emphasis on the Catholic therefore, as this staff member said. These staff members were very familiar with the operational realities and difficulties, as they describe, but they did not have the vocabulary or structure to recognise internal diversity in religion, the impacts of their secular approach, or the intertwined elements of religion, culture, politics, and society. This is what secular reflexivity and religious literacy approaches can offer. When asked whether there should be more on cultural sensitivity, religious literacy, or any other aspects related to this in standards, policies, trainings, and other humanitarian mechanisms, the majority of people I spoke to after Typhoon Haiyan said that it should be kept *ad hoc* so that decisions can be made on the ground about cultural appropriateness. Rather than a lot more training, people wanted an open space for dialogue and a safe space to ask "stupid questions" about secular-religious dynamics and other cultural aspects, as one international staff member put it.

Ager and Ager (2016, p. 104) and Deneulin and Bano (2009, pp. 156–167) also underline this need for spaces of dialogue. Ager and Ager call for voices to:

> critique and to clash – within a safe space of shared interests – if they are to challenge current beliefs and presumptions of global elites rather than simply accommodate them. To create that dialogical engagement – and see shared action agendas emerge by embracing diversity rather than forcing adherence to a discredited, unsustainable modernist agenda – will be to embrace the post-secular age.
>
> (Ager and Ager 2016, p. 104)

This also relates back to Wilson's call for a type of "relational dialogism" that allows for horizontal and vertical, thematic and critical debates to take place about secular-religious dynamics in a "both/and," rather than "either/or" style of thought. Most recently, Wilson has explained that rather than focusing on translation and interpretation, full dialogue must cut across secular and religious categorisations and attend to "broad cross-cutting categories related to how different actors, whether secular, religious, political, social or otherwise, understand the world and consider the best ways for collective life to be organised" (Wilson 2017, p. 14), such as,

> history and time (what are the important historical events/markers for these different actors? How does that affect their view of priorities into the future?); political and societal organisation (What are the rules, values, and principles by which they think collective life together should be organised? How significant is the state, the government, institutions, local societal, and traditional leaders, in the authority structures these actors deem necessary for community?); resources and land (how does this actor or group of actors understand the significance/purpose of land? How is the natural world viewed within the community? As a commodity? As collective or individual property? As sacred? As an influential and powerful agent?); power and authority (what is power within this ontology? What are the main sources of power? What is leadership and how is it defined and constituted?).
>
> (Wilson 2017, p. 14)

These are useful questions that could be the basis of dialogue and relationship-building for secular humanitarian organisations seeking to partner with local faith actors, for example. The Charter for Faith-Based Humanitarian Action also makes a call for a type of post-secular recognition and dialogue, saying:

We call for [faith-based humanitarian] support to be recognised by international and national actors, and government and donor organisations, as a contribution to alleviating needs and the effects of humanitarian crises. We call for constructive dialogue between faith and non-faith players in the larger interest of communities in need.

Fascinatingly, as described previously, localisation provides the perfect space within which these changes can take place. To this extent, I am quite happy to see secular reflexivity and religiously literate approaches as just one part of the shifts that need to take place within the challenge to power that localisation represents. Most notably, psychosocial programming was a particular area in which people felt change was due. A national staff member from an FBO recounted how they used mental health guidance from Sphere which is secular, but found that it did not work for them (although it should be noted that other psychosocial guidance does include religious practices, i.e., Inter-Agency Standing Committee 2007, p. 106). It has generally been found however that recognition of religion in psychosocial humanitarian work is weak (Ager and Ager 2015, pp. 34–35). This FBO started to integrate elements of faith into psychosocial assistance. One of the small things they did was to put up a picture of the Pope hugging a Filipino Cardinal, showing compassion and solidarity towards Filipinos. Two other national staff members for a secular organisation also noted that the area in which they felt a spiritual component was most lacking was psychosocial assistance. One said that you have to reintegrate religion into the IASC Psychosocial Guidelines, which allow for "appropriate communal cultural, spiritual and religious healing practices" (Inter-Agency Standing Committee 2007, p. 106), but must be interpreted in application. An example they gave was reintegrating faith-based ceremonies, notably the ceremonial routine before burying the dead. They said, "We can't just focus on guidelines," adding that they "have to include these parts of the culture." Since these interviews, the Lutheran World Federation joined with Islamic Relief to create a "faith-sensitive" reinterpretation of the IASC guidelines (French *et al.* 2018), which means there is now a religiously literate resource for humanitarians to consult on this matter. There remains a gap for such resources to be developed and used for other humanitarian sectors.

Conclusion

By way of conclusion, it must finally be stated that humanitarian actors are frequently caught between their actions and their reasoning. In order to continue activities, they must abide by donor rules and allow themselves to be swayed, to some extent, by political trends and flows of funding. However, in order to keep the sector alive, the humanitarian reasoning of the past must be examined so that the voices of beneficiaries are accounted for and the dangers of politicisation are minimised. In contexts in which any decision could have dire consequences, the range of mainstreamed concerns is overwhelming, with climate change adaptation, gender, land reform, and disaster risk reduction only some of the policy concerns that humanitarians must keep in mind. The introduction of secular-religious dynamics as yet another area of concern may be unpopular in light of these other, already existing pressures. Yet, the literature has consistently pointed towards the fact that, both historically and in the present day, these dynamics have influenced and will continue to influence humanitarian action. Likewise, we have seen throughout these preceding chapters the ways in which secularity continues to hold a powerful sway. New humanitarian trends, such as localisation, are ripe for leading with ideas of secular reflexivity and religious literacy to see how best to work on equitable relationships between partners and towards an appreciation of "both/and" secular-religious dynamics.

Bibliography

Ager, A., and Ager, J., 2011. Faith and the Discourse of Secular Humanitarianism. *Journal of Refugee Studies*, 24 (3), 456–472.

Ager, A., and Ager J., 2015. *Faith, Secularism, and Humanitarian Engagement: Finding the Place of Religion in the Support of Displaced Communities*. New York: Palgrave Macmillan.

Ager, A., and Ager, J., 2016. Sustainable Development and Religion: Accommodating Diversity in a Post-Secular Age. *The Review of Faith & International Affairs*, 14 (3), 101–105. Available from: https://doi.org/10.1080/15570274.2016.1215813.

Ager, W., Ager, A., and Horn, R., 2018. A Faith-Sensitive Approach in Humanitarian Response. *Islamic Relief Worldwide*, Lutheran World Federation. Available from: https://refugee.jliflc.com/resources/a-faith-sensitive-approach-in-humanitarian-response/.

Atalay, Z., 2019. Partners in Patriarchy: Faith-Based Organizations and Neoliberalism in Turkey. *Critical Sociology*, 45 (3), 431–445. Available from: https://doi.org/10.1177/0896920517711488.

Barnett, M., and Weiss T., 2011. *Humanitarianism Contested: Where Angels Fear to Tread*. Routledge Global Institutions 51. London: Routledge.

Beckford, J.A., 2012. SSSR Presidential Address Public Religions and the Postsecular: Critical Reflections. *Journal for the Scientific Study of Religion,* 51 (1), 1–19. Available from: https://doi.org/10.1111/j.1468-5906.2011.01625.x.

Berger, P., 2014. *The Many Altars of Modernity: Toward a Paradigm for Religion in a Pluralist Age*. Walter de Gruyter GmbH & Co KG.

Bush, R., Fountain, P., and Feener, R.M., 2015. Introduction. *In: Religion and the Politics of Development*, 1–9. International Political Economy Series. London: Palgrave Macmillan. Available from: https://doi.org/10.1057/9781137438577_1.

CARE, Christian Aid, Tearfund, ActionAid, CAFOD, and Oxfam. 2019. *Accelerating Localisation through Partnerships: Recommendations for Operational Practices That Strengthen the Leadership of National and Local Actors in Partnership-Based Humanitarian Action in South Sudan*. Available from: https://reliefweb.int/sites/reliefweb.int/files/resources/Accelerating%20Localisa tion%20Research%20Summary_SouthSudan.pdf.

Charter 4 Change. 2015. Charter for Change: Localisation of Humanitarian Aid. *Text. Catholic Agency for Overseas Development (CAFOD)*. Available from: http://reliefweb.int/report/world/charter-change-localisation-humanitarian-aid.

Cloke, P., 2011. Emerging Postsecular Rapprochement in the Contemporary City. *In:* C. Baker, and J. Beaumont, eds. *Postsecular Cities: Space, Theory and Practice*. London: Continuum, 237–253.

Cloke, P., and Beaumont, J., 2013. Geographies of Postsecular Rapprochement in the City. *Progress in Human Geography*, 37 (1), 27–51.

De Geoffroy, V., Grunewald, F., and Chéilleachair, R.N., 2017. More than the Money – Localisation in Practice. *URD*, Trocaire. Available from: www.trocaire. org/sites/default/files/resources/policy/more-than-the-money-localisation-in-practice.pdf.

Deneulin, S., and Bano, M., 2009. *Religion in Development: Rewriting the Secular Script*. London: Zed.

Dillon, M., 2010. 2009 Association for the Sociology of Religion Presidential Address: Can Post-Secular Society Tolerate Religious Differences? *Sociology of Religion*, 71 (2), 139–156.

Eade, D., 1997. *Capacity-Building: An Approach to People-Centred Development*. Oxfam.

Evans, B., and Reid, J., 2014. *Resilient Life: The Art of Living Dangerously*. 1st ed. Cambridge: Polity.

Featherstone, A., 2014. *Missed Again: Making Space for Partnership in the Typhoon Haiyan Response*. London: Christian Aid; CAFOD; Oxfam GB; Tearfund; Action Aid.

Fiddian-Qasmiyeh, E., 2011. The Pragmatics of Performance: Putting 'Faith' in Aid in the Sahrawi Refugee Camps. *Journal of Refugee Studies*, 24 (3), 533–547.

Fiddian-Qasmiyeh, E., 2015. Conflicting Missions? The Politics of Evangelical Humanitarianism in the Sahrawi and Palestinian Protracted Refugee Situations. *In: Building Noah's Ark for Migrants, Refugees, and Religious Communities*. Contemporary Anthropology of Religion. New York: Palgrave Macmillan, 157–179.

Flanigan, S.T., 2009. *For the Love of God: NGOs and Religious Identity in a Violent World*. Sterling, VA: Kumarian Press.

Fountain, P., 2011. Review of Shawn Teresa Flanigan (2010) 'For the Love of God: NGOs and Religious Identity in a Violent World' (Sterling, VA, Kumarian). *Transformation: An International Journal of Holistic Mission Studies*.

French, M., Fiztgibbon, A., Ager, W., Ager, A., and Horn, R., 2018. A Faith-Sensitive Approach in Humanitarian Response. *Islamic Relief Worldwide*, Lutheran World Federation. https://refugee.jliflc.com/resources/a-faith-sensitive-approach-in-humani tarian-response/.

Habermas, J., 2006. Religion in the Public Sphere. *European Journal of Philosophy* 14 (1): 1–25.

Habermas, J., 2008. Notes on Post-Secular Society. *New Perspective Quarterly (NPQ)*, Fall, 17–29.

Hanley, T., Binas, R., Murray, J., and Tribunalo, B., 2014. IASC Inter-Agency Humanitarian Evaluation of the Typhoon Haiyan Response. *Inter-Agency Humanitarian Evaluation Steering Group*. New York: UNOCHA. Available from: www. unicef.org/evaldatabase/index_78200.html.

Hopgood, S., and Vinjamuri, L., 2012. Faith in Markets. *In*: Janice Gross Stein, ed. *Sacred Aid: Faith and Humanitarianism*. New York: Oxford University Press, Inc., 38–64.

Hurd, E.S., 2015. *Beyond Religious Freedom: The New Global Politics of Religion*. Princeton, NJ: Princeton University Press. Available from: http://press.princeton. edu/titles/10626.html.

Inter-Agency Standing Committee, 2007. "IASC Guidelines on Mental Health and Psychosocial Support in Emergency Settings." Geneva: Inter-Agency Standing Committee. http://www.who.int/mental_health/emergencies/guidelines_iasc_ mental_health_psychosocial_june_2007.pdf.

Inter-Agency Standing Committee. 2018. Grand Bargain. *Inter-Agency Standing Committee*, April 14, 2018. Available from: https://interagencystandingcommit tee.org/grand-bargain-hosted-iasc.

Junker-Kenny, M., 2011. *Habermas and Theology. Philosophy and Theology*. London: T & T Clark.

Karam, A., 2018. Deconstructing and Reconstructing Secular Approaches to Religion in Multilateral Settings. *In:* M. Garred, and M. Abu-Nimer, eds. *Making Peace with Faith*. Lanham; Boulder; New York; London: Rowman & Littlefield.

Karam, A., 2019. Religion & Development: An Enhanced Approach or a Transaction? *Inter Press Service*, April 12, 2019. Available from: www.ipsnews. net/2019/04/religion-development-enhanced-approach-transaction/.

Lynch, C., and Schwarz, T., 2017. Humanitarianism's Proselytism Problem. *International Studies Quarterly*, 60 (4). Available from: www.isanet.org/Publications/ ISQ/Posts/ID/5271/Humanitarianisms-Proselytism-Problem.

Mahmood, S., 2011. *Politics of Piety: The Islamic Revival and the Feminist Subject*. Reissue ed. Princeton, NJ: Princeton University Press.

Mahmood, S., 2015. *Religious Difference in a Secular Age: A Minority Report*. Princeton: Princeton University Press.

Mahmood, S., 2016. Religious Difference in a Secular Age: A Minority Report – An Introduction. *The Immanent Frame* (blog). February 9, 2016. http://blogs. ssrc.org/tif/2016/02/09/religious-difference-in-a-secular-age-a-minority-report- an-introduction/.

Mavelli, L., and Petito, F., 2014a. Towards a Postsecular International Politics. *In:* L. Mavelli, and F. Petito, eds. *Towards a Postsecular International Politics: New Forms of Community, Identity, and Power*. Basingstoke; Hampshire: Palgrave Macmillan, 1–28.

Mavelli, L., and Petito, F., eds., 2014b. Towards a Postsecular International Politics: New Forms of Community, Identity, and Power. *Culture and Religion in International Relations*. Basingstoke; Hampshire: Palgrave Macmillan.

Mendieta, E., 2010. A Post-Secular World Society? On the Philosophical Post-Secular Consciousness and the Multicultural World Society. An Interview with Jurgen Habermas. Translated by Matthias Fritsch. *The Immanent Frame* (blog). http://blogs.ssrc.org/tif/2010/02/03/a-postsecular-world-society/.

Merli, C., 2012. Religion and Disaster in Anthropological Research. *In:* M. Kearnes, F. Klauser, and S. Lane, eds. *Critical Risk Research.* John Wiley & Sons, Ltd., 43–58.

Metcalfe-Hough, V., Fenton, W., and Poole, L., 2019. *Grand Bargain Annual Independent Report 2019.* London: ODI Humanitarian Policy Group. https://interagencystandingcommittee.org/system/files/grand_bargain_annual_independent_report_0.pdf.

Moore, D., 2015. Our Method: Religious Literacy Project. *Religious Literacy Project*, Harvard Divinity School. https://rlp.hds.harvard.edu/files/hds-rlp/files/rlp_method_2015.pdf.

Ramalingam, B., Gray, B., and Cerruti, G., 2013. Missed Opportunities: The Case for Strengthening Nationa and Local Partnership-Based Humanitarian Responses. *Research.* ActionAid; CAFOD; Christian Aid; Oxfam GB; Tearfund. www.alnap.org/resource/8890.

Sanderson, D., and Delica-Willison, Z., 2014. Philippines Typhoon Haiyan: Response Review. *Disasters Emergency Committee.* Humanitarian Coalition.

Tamminga, P., and Redheffer, M., 2014. Certification Review Project: Reviewing the Draft Certification Model: A Case Study in the Philippines. *Steering Committee for Humanitarian Response.*

Tanner, L., and Moro, L., 2016. *Missed Out: The Role of Local Actors in the Humanitarian Response in the South Sudan Conflict.* Oxfam GB, CAFOD and Trócaire in partnership, Christian Aid, Tearfund. Available from: http://hdl.handle.net/10546/606290.

Thomas, S., 2000. "Taking Religious and Cultural Pluralism Seriously: The Global Resurgence of Religion and the Transformation of International Society." *Millennium – Journal of International Studies* 29: 815–41.

Tomalin, E., 2015. Gender, Development, and the 'De-Privatisation' of Religion: Reframing Feminism and Religion in Asia. *In: Religion and the Politics of Development.* International Political Economy Series. London: Palgrave Macmillan, 61–82. Available from: https://doi.org/10.1057/9781137438577_4.

UN Inter-Agency Task Force for Engaging with Faith-Based Organisations. 2016. *Religious Resourcing for Humanitarian Efforts: Highlights from a Policy Roundtable in Preparation for the World Humanitarian Summit (WHS).* New York: United Nations. Available from: www.agendaforhumanity.org/sites/default/files/WHS%20Religious%20Resourcing%20-%20Highlights.pdf.

UNSG. 2016a. *Chair's Summary by the United Nations Secretary General. Standing Up for Humanity: Committing to Action.* New York: United Nations. Available from: www.agendaforhumanity.org/sites/default/files/resources/2017/Jul/Chair%27s_Summary.pdf.

UNSG, 2016b. *One Humanity: Shared Responsibility | Report of the UN Secretary-General for the World Humanitarian Summit.* New York: United Nations. Available from: www.alnap.org/resource/21845.

UNSG, 2016c. *Outcome of the World Humanitarian Summit: Report of the Secretary-General.* Available from: www.agendaforhumanity.org/sites/default/files/A-71-

353%20-%20SG%20Report%20on%20the%20Outcome%20of%20the%20 WHS.pdf.

Urquhart, A., and Tuchel, L., 2018. *Global Humanitarian Assistance Report 2018*. Bristol: Development Initiatives. Available from: http://devinit.org/post/ global-humanitarian-assistance-report-2018/.

Wall, I., and Hedlund, K., 2016. Localisation and Locally-Led Crisis Response: A Literature Review. *Local 2 Global Protection; Swiss Agency for Development and Cooperation*. Available from: www.local2global.info/wp-content/uploads/ L2GP_SDC_Lit_Review_LocallyLed_June_2016_final.pdf.

Wilkinson, O., 2018a. When Local Faith Actors Meet Localisation. *Refugee Hosts* (blog). February 7, 2018. Available from: https://refugeehosts.org/2018/02/07/ when-local-faith-actors-meet-localisation/.

Wilkinson, O., 2018b. Secular Humanitarians and the Postsecular: Reflections on Habermas and the Typhoon Haiyan Disaster Response. *Journal of Contemporary Religion*, 33 (2), 193–208. Available from: https://doi.org/10.1080/13537903. 2018.1469260.

Wilkinson, O., and Ager, J., 2017. *Scoping Study on Local Faith Communities in Urban Displacement: Evidence on Localisation and Urbanisation*. Washington, DC: Joint Learning Initiative on Faith and Local Communities.

Wilson, E.K., 2012. *After Secularism: Rethinking Religion in Global Politics*. Basingstoke: Palgrave Macmillan.

Wilson, E.K., 2014. Faith-Based Organizations and Postsecularism in Contemporary International Relations. *In:* L. Mavelli, and F. Petito, eds. *Towards a Postsecular International Politics: New Forms of Community, Identity, and Power*. Culture and Religion in International Relations. Basingstoke, Hampshire: Palgrave Macmillan, 219–242.

Wilson, E.K., 2017. 'Power Differences' and 'the Power of Difference': The Dominance of Secularism as Ontological Injustice. *Globalizations*, 14 (7), 1076–1093. Available from: https://doi.org/10.1080/14747731.2017.1308062.

World Humanitarian Summit. 2016a. Charter for Faith-Based Humaitarian Action. *Istanbul*, Turkey: United Nations. Available from: www.agendaforhumanity.org/ initiatives/4012.

World Humanitarian Summit. 2016b. *Commitments to Action*. New York: United Nations. Available from: www.agendaforhumanity.org/sites/default/files/resources/ 2017/Jul/WHS_Commitment_to_Action_8September2016.pdf.

6 Conclusion

This book started with two fairly contrary positions from humanitarian workers – one saying that religion was always part of their work and the other saying that it was never part of their work. Over the course of this book, I have made the case that these outwardly contrary perspectives can exist within the secular humanitarian system as part of the secular-religious dynamics that serve to promote some discourses and marginalise others. In many ways, this has been an analysis of power balances and how secular justifications have allowed for certain boundary-making that asserts the hierarchical position of some decision-makers in the humanitarian system over other humanitarian staff. My aim is not to isolate secular-religious dynamics as the only influencing factor in contemporary humanitarian power imbalances but to demonstrate how it is one part of the ways in which the system demarcates conceptual territory and subordinates some over others. It is no surprise, therefore, that the two humanitarians from the examples at the very beginning of the book are also representative of other divides in the humanitarian system: national staff and international staff, community-facing positions and managerial decision-making positions, Global North and Global South, long-term presence and short-term deployments. These divides are known and debated in the humanitarian system. This book has made the case throughout that secular-religious dynamics are an often ignored or unrecognised aspect of these humanitarian power imbalances.

The first two chapters laid out the conceptual background to this argument. Secularising forces such as the diminishment of religious authority, the privatisation of religion, and the pluralisation of options mark some of the bounds of what can be seen as aspects of the secular. Yet it was also in understanding that the secular is not neutral – it is a socially constructed topic with its own value system – that we can see the ways in which secularity can be used and abused to wield power, just as religions have been similarly used. While it is useful to look at the parameters of the secular, ultimately it is a secular-religious dynamic that is of interest, recognising that secularity aims to make religions seem "other" when, in fact, secular and religious concepts are co-constitutive and mutually dependent in many ways. The categories must be seen as highly intertwined rather than distinct and clashing.

Just as the secular-religious dynamics are socially constructed, vulnerability to disasters and the level of disaster impacts are affected by social influences. While backing away from the notion that religious beliefs and practices are for the poor and secularity is for those who feel secure (i.e., the rich) (Norris and Inglehart 2011), we see that the humanitarian system represents a context in which much of the decision-making power is held in more secularised societies and humanitarian response is often located in areas where religiosity is high. Humanitarian work is understood as a complex system with emergent norms, non-linear processes, and an historical evolution. The evolution of the humanitarian system neither shows a neat story of secularisation nor one of religious resurgence. Instead, throughout the evolution of the humanitarian system there have been secular-religious dynamics at play, with secularity playing a dominant role in higher-level decision-making, yet equally religious beliefs and practices being encountered by humanitarians on a daily basis in work around the world. By analysing humanitarian ethics, principles, and organisational typologies as constitutive parts of the humanitarian system, we saw that a secularised notion of humanity, ethics based within the immanent frame of this world, technical and material foci aside from spiritual and holistic version of human life, privatised and marginalised religious beliefs and practices, and instrumentalising and power wielding (by boundary and decision-making) forces are all part of secularity in the humanitarian system.

Focusing on the humanitarian response to Typhoon Haiyan, it is vital to understand the ways in which religious beliefs and practices are a current part of people's lives in the Visayan region of the Philippines and how those beliefs and practices influence their perspective not only of disasters but also of the humanitarian system. Religious experience influenced people's culture, practice, relationship, and identity following the typhoon. It was part of their meaning making, social connection, grounding in tradition, ritual, and familiarity, and ideas about their place in the world in relation to overarching concepts such as climate change. As frequently stated in FGDs, these are the elements that help people "cope up," or, translated into NGO language, build their disaster resilience. Religious beliefs did not lead to purely fatalistic worldviews and actions. Humanitarian organisations were seen to be part of God's plan. Humanitarian organisations that recognised the importance of these aspects of life were respected, yet the faith-base or secularity of the organisation in the immediate emergency period ultimately did not matter.

It was in the weeks and months after the immediate emergency that differences started to arise. For people affected by Haiyan, the secular was associated with short-term programmes, little interaction with the organisations, a focus on the material alone, a lack of impartiality and transparency, and questions around trustworthiness. Conversely, for humanitarian staff, the markers of secularity were no proselytisation, a secular organisational mission and vision, a focus on efficiency and bureaucracy, little mention (if at all) of religion in programmes (marginalisation of religion/religion as taboo), impartiality and neutrality, a broadly secular workplace environment (privatised religion), boundaries about the level to which they would participate in beneficiaries' religiosity, and respectfulness, which had hallmarks of the instrumentalisation of religion due to power imbalances about who the respectfulness served. These differing perspectives have little in common. In fact, some points, especially around impartiality, are directly contradictory. Talal Asad's criticism of secularity as inherently non-neutral encompasses humanitarian notions of impartiality and neutrality as well. The argument he puts forwards underlines that secularity does not guarantee tolerance and is inherently political. The present results point towards this problem of impartiality and neutrality for secular humanitarians as well. While trying to maintain these principles as a secular ideal, it was admitted with neutrality that it is often an unachievable ideal and political affiliations are common. Yet impartiality remained a central tenet of secularity for humanitarians, even if beneficiaries did not feel they achieved this aim. The fact that impartiality is still seen as a defining point of difference for humanitarians underlines the dominance of secularity in the humanitarian system.

For affected people, one of the most frequently mentioned effects of a secular approach was the result of a focus on timeliness and efficiency: little interaction between organisations and beneficiaries. As summed up by one respondent, this was the "How are you?" gap. It seems that in privatising religion and culture and emphasising the technological and the bureaucratic in line with secularisation theories, secular humanitarian organisations have lost an element of the social and personal in their interactions. This was the effect of functional secularism across the humanitarian system and it affected any organisation, be they secular or faith-based, which tried to fit into the norms of this system. The notable outcome of this observation is that there should be a differentiation between the functional secularism of the humanitarian system and the secularity of individual organisations. While the secular system may prioritise timeliness, it is open for individual secular organisations to increase their micro-level interactions with beneficiaries and close the "How are you?" gap.

No proselytisation does not mean no religion. In general, it conveyed the idea that you cannot use humanitarian action to preach or try to convert people to a religion. Yet other elements of faith are allowed in the secular humanitarian system. This was the boundary, for example, between allowing community members to lead a prayer if they wanted versus an NGO leading the community in prayer before distribution of relief goods. The former was allowed, the latter was not. This conveys a secular morality in which pluralistic forms of religious expression are allowed for others, but it is not appropriate for the secular actor to instigate this expression. It is secular in that there is a clear differentiation between secular and religious ways of operating and it affirms that secular actors cannot spread religious aims. While not furthering religious decline in this way (it is not secularisation), it ensures that the secular actors remain separate from religious growth.

Within a hierarchy of worth in the secular humanitarian organisations, religious beliefs and practices hold very low or non-existent standing. Staff members accept that any religious beliefs they may hold should be kept out of the workplace. Furthermore, the removal of religious areas of life from the organisation mean that it is focused on less ethereal and more tangible elements of experience, as one respondent revealed when saying that their secular mandate meant they were a "purely technical organisation." The focus on efficiency and bureaucracy for secular organisations again highlights the centrality of material and tangible experience as part of a secular humanitarian ethic. Targets and speed in achieving those targets is central to this characteristic. These are the technical criteria which show that religious principles or notions of success are displaced in the humanitarian system. Organisations have technical foci and use technical criteria to measure success, echoing Redfield's (2012) conception of the secular value of life in humanitarianism. We are reminded that the definition of the secular focuses on precisely this: that the secular is everything of this world, temporal, material, and profane. This technical and material focus denotes a secular approach in that it focuses on what is important for "human flourishing" within this world, as Taylor (Taylor 2007, p. 20) puts it. Therefore, secular humanitarianism justifies its material focus within a rationality that sees the extent of human experience happening within a tangible and material world. This characteristic intersects with another commonly cited element of secularisation: bureaucratisation. The push for efficiency is at once balanced by the ingrained bureaucracy of humanitarian relief (as results also showed that people struggled with much red tape), with both being indicative of the secular aspects of the humanitarian system.

Secular-religious dynamics in a humanitarian response is a process of boundary-making, with secular humanitarians using secular justifications, such as those from the principles, to define the boundaries, while also feeling the push and pull of the need to be culturally sensitive and wondering how to achieve this balance. Ultimately, this is not a critique of the actions of individual secular humanitarian actors who are often juggling these tensions and making *ad hoc* decisions that allow for religious beliefs and practices. For example, most secular organisations were willing to participate in religious ceremonies if asked by beneficiaries or local staff. The evidence of the secular was apparent not in when they participated, but where they drew boundaries. Prayer is fine, but not too much. Participation in religious ceremonies is fine but building a church or altars in shelters is not. Respectfulness allowed for cooperation, but the boundaries dictated by this secular respect meant that religion remained largely privatised and marginalised. This meant that people in secular organisations were wary of working with religious institutions, such as churches, even if they would not evangelise in their programme. This reluctance meant that opportunities for partnerships with religious institutions were not taken or progressed. A lot more reflection and negotiation of secular and religious boundaries are evidenced in interaction with beneficiaries and it is at this point that the reflexivity necessary for a more post-secular approach to humanitarian action was at times present.

It was in Chapter 5, therefore, that an approach for self-reflection and learning within secular humanitarian spheres was proposed. Following from current humanitarian trends from the World Humanitarian Summit and aligned to localisation, it became clear that current interests in religions are still within the parameters of secular boundary-making and power imbalances, even while there are good intentions to understand more. While a religious literacy approach can help secular humanitarians understand more, it should also be coupled with self-reflection from humanitarians along the lines of post-secular reflexivity. An approach of secular reflexivity is suggested precisely because it does not pose radical realignment for secular humanitarians – they remain secular yet open themselves to processes of complementary learning and to refraining from the quick imposition of boundaries. The "ask" of secular humanitarians is that they take the time to engage with the religious beliefs of others, noting that this is inherently worthwhile and not in contradiction to the humanitarian principles.

These processes are starting to change. I have, this year, been involved in two such projects that include elements of religious literacy with and between the humanitarian system and local faith actors. While a few trainings will not make system-wide change, they are indicative of a growing awareness, brought on by the realities of localisation, of the need to understand local faith actors and how to partner with them. Local faith actors are, in some contexts, the majority of local actors. There is a burden on them to learn the secular parameters of the humanitarian system and confine themselves to these parameters. There are local faith actors successfully accomplishing this around the world. They are respected and legitimate local partners for the secular humanitarian system. Yet the imbalance remains wherein the secular humanitarian system has not considered the extent of this burden on local faith actors and even their own local staff to act as culture brokers. Instead, there is a need for the secular humanitarian system to realise the culture *it* brings to any context and part of that is the influence and power of secular-religious dynamics.

In conclusion, the evidence on the secular humanitarian system has shown that an "ignorance is bliss" approach to secular-religious dynamics in disaster-affected communities is not a neutral position and that the boundaries created by secular humanitarians allow religious beliefs and practices to be demonstrated only in tokenistic fashion in the public sphere created by external humanitarians following a disaster. Arguing for increased reflexivity among secular humanitarians, this book has acknowledged increased recent interest in religions but warns that localised humanitarian response will not be achieved without fully contending with intersecting areas of contention between humanitarians and local communities, of which secular-religious dynamics is one part.

Bibliography

Norris, P., and Inglehart, R., 2011. *Sacred and Secular: Religion and Politics Worldwide*. 2nd ed. Cambridge: Cambridge University Press.

Redfield, P., 2012. Secular Humanitarianism and the Value of Life. *In: What Matters? Ethnographies of Value in a not so Secular Age*. New York: Columbia University Press, 144–178.

Taylor, C., 2007. *A Secular Age*. Harvard: Harvard University Press.

Index

For Product Safety Concerns and Information please contact our EU
representative GPSR@taylorandfrancis.com
Taylor & Francis Verlag GmbH, Kaufingerstraße 24, 80331 München, Germany